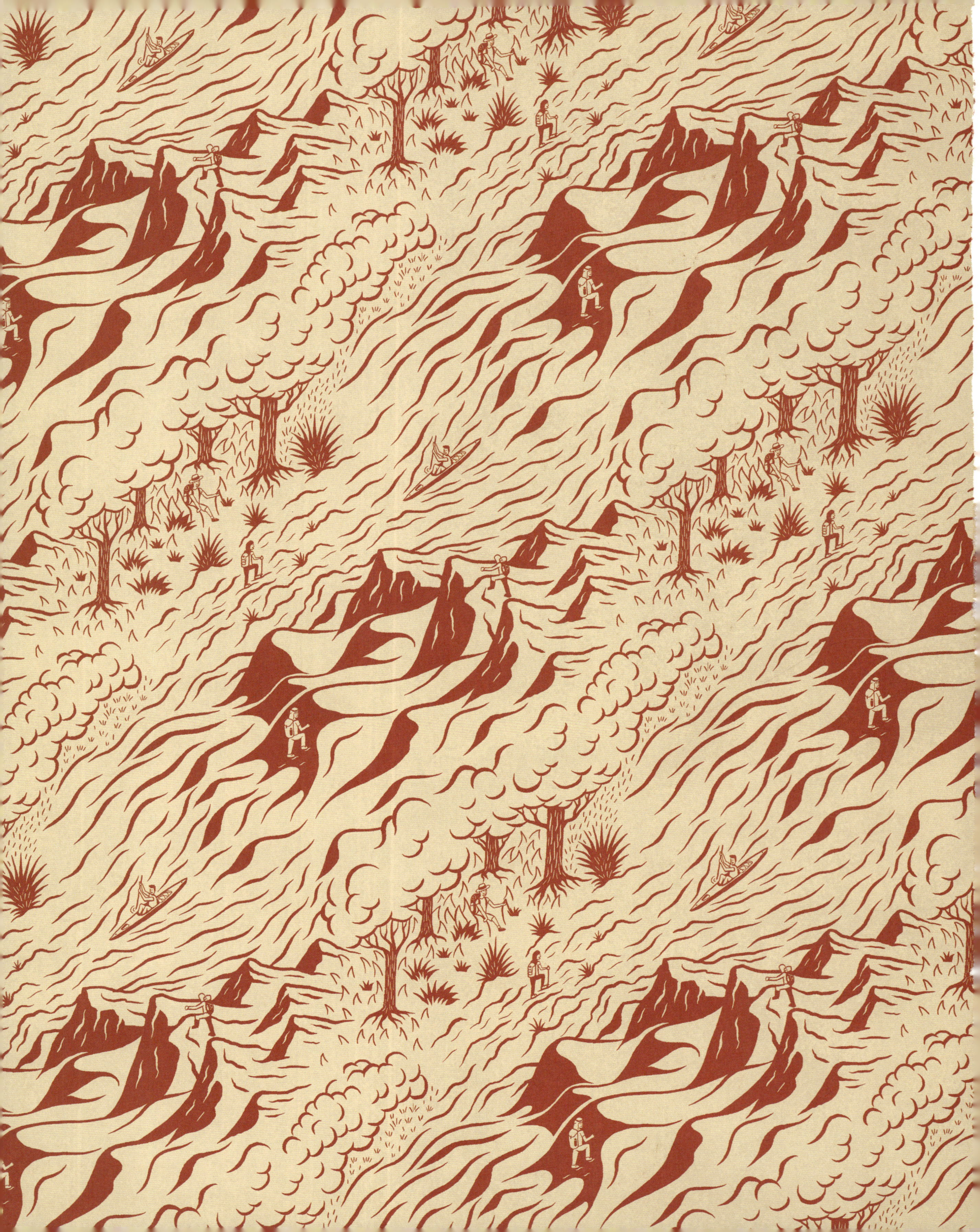

DISCOVERY. ADVENTURE. DANGER. ENDURANCE.

INCREDIBLE JOURNEYS

ILLUSTRATED BY
SAM BREWSTER

LEVISON WOOD

wren
&rook

For my Mum and Dad,
who inspired me to follow my dreams. – L.W.

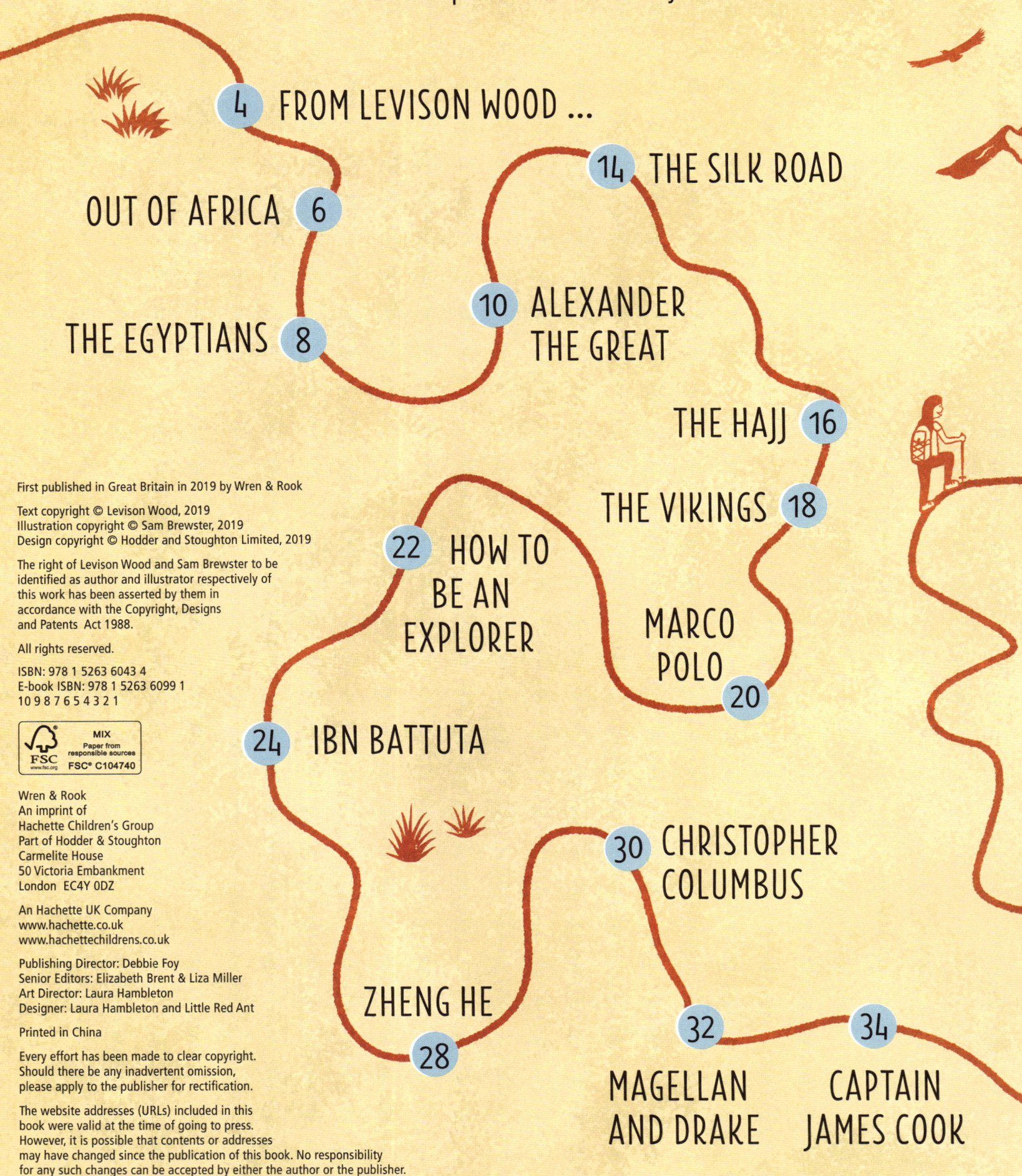

- 4 FROM LEVISON WOOD ...
- 14 THE SILK ROAD
- 6 OUT OF AFRICA
- 10 ALEXANDER THE GREAT
- 8 THE EGYPTIANS
- 16 THE HAJJ
- 18 THE VIKINGS
- 22 HOW TO BE AN EXPLORER
- 20 MARCO POLO
- 24 IBN BATTUTA
- 30 CHRISTOPHER COLUMBUS
- 28 ZHENG HE
- 32 MAGELLAN AND DRAKE
- 34 CAPTAIN JAMES COOK

First published in Great Britain in 2019 by Wren & Rook

Text copyright © Levison Wood, 2019
Illustration copyright © Sam Brewster, 2019
Design copyright © Hodder and Stoughton Limited, 2019

The right of Levison Wood and Sam Brewster to be identified as author and illustrator respectively of this work has been asserted by them in accordance with the Copyright, Designs and Patents Act 1988.

All rights reserved.
ISBN: 978 1 5263 6043 4
E-book ISBN: 978 1 5263 6099 1
10 9 8 7 6 5 4 3 2 1

MIX
Paper from responsible sources
FSC® C104740

Wren & Rook
An imprint of
Hachette Children's Group
Part of Hodder & Stoughton
Carmelite House
50 Victoria Embankment
London EC4Y 0DZ

An Hachette UK Company
www.hachette.co.uk
www.hachettechildrens.co.uk

Publishing Director: Debbie Foy
Senior Editors: Elizabeth Brent & Liza Miller
Art Director: Laura Hambleton
Designer: Laura Hambleton and Little Red Ant

Printed in China

Every effort has been made to clear copyright. Should there be any inadvertent omission, please apply to the publisher for rectification.

The website addresses (URLs) included in this book were valid at the time of going to press. However, it is possible that contents or addresses may have changed since the publication of this book. No responsibility for any such changes can be accepted by either the author or the publisher.

THE INCREDIBLE JOURNEYS

BURTON, SPEKE AND BAKER — 44

LEWIS AND CLARK — 38

46 THE HEART OF AFRICA

42 TRAILBLAZERS

48 NELLIE BLY

50 TO THE POLES

WOMEN IN THE MIDDLE EAST — 52

40 CHARLES DARWIN

62 THE DEEP

AMELIA EARHART — 54

60 INTO SPACE

58 MOUNT EVEREST

INDEX — 64

Acknowledgements

Thank you to all the people who helped me along the way with my adventures, to my late grandparents who fuelled my curiosity about the world, and to those teachers who gave me the courage and confidence to go and explore. Thank you to Jo Cantello, my wonderful agent; Charlotte Tottenham for her help with the research and editorial; Sam Brewster for the beautiful illustrations; and all the team at Wren & Rook for their hard work in making this book a reality.

FROM LEVISON WOOD ...

When I was young, I dreamed of travelling the world. I used to stare out of my bedroom window and look across the garden fence towards the fields and beyond where the woods were. I imagined that further still, beyond the woods, there was a land completely unexplored. A place full of wild animals and beasts that even my parents didn't know. I wanted to explore this place of my imagination and to see what it was really like.

I began to read about places far away from my home. About other countries and cultures across the ages. I discovered prehistoric cave people and ancient Greeks and strange warriors called Vikings with long hair and longships. I imagined what it must have been like to travel in those days, before airplanes were invented, when it took days, weeks or even months to get anywhere. I read about the famous men and women who led these people, including Alexander the Great, who rode an ebony horse across all of Asia. I imagined myself on a horse, travelling through mountain passes, deserts and jungles.

I learned about people through the ages who made great voyages too, such as Captain Cook, who sailed by ship to the far reaches of the oceans, and Amelia Earhart, who flew to distant lands in some of the first aeroplanes. But I wondered if there was anywhere left to explore in this modern world of ours.

As a child I loved camping, and I used to pretend that my garden was a steamy tropical jungle. I dreamed that one day I might camp in a real one, like the explorers I read about. I promised myself that as soon as I was old enough, I would embark on my own adventures – and that's exactly what I did!

I finished school aged eighteen and set off, following in the footsteps of my heroes. I saw savannahs in Africa, deserts in Australia, mountains in the Himalayas and jungles in India. In fact, I had so many incredible adventures that I decided to become an explorer.

But I soon realised it wasn't that easy. You need to know so much to be an explorer, and have experience in many different things, so I carried on with my studies and learned even more about history and geography and exploration. But I always took the time to travel whenever I could, because I wanted to see the world for myself. Just like the very first humans, who decided to leave their caves and venture into the unknown, I too was curious to see what was out there, and not to settle for other people's stories. I wanted to have stories of my own!

And now I do. Since those early travels, I've been lucky enough to visit 100 countries all around the world. I've walked across Africa, trekked the frontiers of Europe and traversed the Silk Road in the wake of Marco Polo. I've camped for months in jungles and walked across the Sahara Desert. I've voyaged across oceans and seen some pretty weird and wonderful things along the way. But I'll never forget how important it is to dream and to read.

I hope you're inspired by this book, and the stories of all these brave men and women who were pioneers of exploration. All of these journeys were incredible for different reasons — because they were awe-inspiring and magnificent, or because they were incredible in length, duration and scope.

One thing's for sure — there are lots of places still left to explore! This world is a big place, and there are a lot of other worlds to discover too.

Who knows where your inspiration will take you?

5

OUT OF AFRICA   A JOURNEY INTO THE UNKNOWN

6 30–15,000 years ago
Our ancestors crossed a land bridge that used to link Asia and North America. They survived by eating fruits, nuts, seeds and vegetables. They also hunted wild and ferocious animals like sabre-toothed tigers and mastodons, eating the meat and wearing the animal fur.

7 Fossils of the ancient creatures they ate have been found all over the world – a fossilised mastodon was even discovered under a motorway in San Diego, USA!

Humans are capable of incredible things. I've walked 6,400 km through Africa, travelled 8,000 km around the Arabian Peninsula and hiked the 2,700-km length of the Himalayas. But this is nothing compared to the feats of exploration of the very first people to live on Earth.

Two million years ago, our ancestors – very early species of human with names like *Homo erectus* – evolved in Africa but began to walk out of the continent, hunting and living in caves along the way. Every day was a battle for survival as they struggled to keep warm and safe, and to find food.

It took hundreds of thousands of years for people to populate the whole world. Meanwhile, the species *Homo erectus* evolved into *Homo sapiens* – our direct ancestors. Incredibly, most people alive today are related to just one *Homo sapiens* family who left Africa about 125,000 years ago. Their descendents, who roamed around the world with no equipment, were the first real explorers. This map shows what the Earth looked like about 18,000 years ago, during the middle of an ice age.

8 30,000 years ago
Humans reached South America. Every day was a fight for survival, and keeping warm was often the hardest battle. Eventually, they discovered fire – and life changed forever. Hearths have been found in ancient houses at Pedra Furada, in Brazil, from those very early fires.

EUROPE

2 **50,000 years ago**
The first humans made their own weapons and stone tools to hunt animals and build homes. Some very early tools have been discovered at Yuanmou, in China.

5 **40,000 years ago**
Early humans moved into Europe. In Lascaux, France, you can see cave paintings which are 24,000 years old! They suggest that our ancestors decorated their homes with beautiful art.

ASIA

1 **60,000 years ago**
Our *Homo sapiens* ancestors started moving out of Africa towards Arabia, in modern-day Asia.

AFRICA

Start

3 For thousands of years, early humans lived in forests like the apes they evolved from. But as time went on, they lived in all kinds of places – trees, caves, and even huts made of reeds, bones, wood, straw or animal skins!

AUSTRALIA

4 **60–40,000 years ago**
Our ancestors travelled to Australia from south-east Asia, but no one is really sure how. Historians think they may have used bamboo rafts.

9 At the time early people were walking out of Africa, Antarctica was covered in an enormous ice sheet. Humans didn't reach Antarctica until the nineteenth century!

KEY
ICE SHEETS
LAND BRIDGES THAT USED TO EXIST

THE EGYPTIANS
THE PATH OF A CIVILISATION

LOCATION MAP

MESOPOTAMIA

ARABIA

Mediterranean Sea

GIZA

1 Cleopatra (69–30 BCE) was one of the most famous ancient Egyptian leaders. She was a great queen, and very rich and beautiful, but she was also very greedy. In 31 BCE, she went to war against the Romans and lost, which led to the collapse of ancient Egyptian civilisation. It is said that she committed suicide by allowing a poisonous snake to bite her.

2 The Egyptians travelled to neighbouring regions, such as Mesopotamia and Arabia, to trade stone, pottery, papyrus, dried fish and lentils.

3 When wealthy Egyptians died they were buried in vast pyramid tombs, which you can still see in parts of Egypt today. The pyramids at Giza tower over the desert, but some ancient Egyptian tombs, like the ones I visited in modern-day Sudan, are so submerged in sand it is almost impossible to see them.

4 Every year, the River Nile flooded, and the enterprising Egyptians used the water to drink and to irrigate their fields. The rich, fertile land and the water supply attracted more and more brave explorers from across Africa.

8

LUXOR TEMPLE

DEIR-EL-MEDINA

WILD RIVER
The Nile is home to an amazing variety of animals, including crocodiles and hippos.

ABU SIMBEL

SACRED PETS
The ancient Egyptians kept many animals — cows, goats, pigs, ducks, even geese! They believed that cats and scarab beetles were sacred and lucky.

KUSH

Red Sea

⑤ Deir-el-Medina is a ruined village on the west bank of the Nile. There are some amazing remains of ancient Egyptian homes there, preserved in the burning heat of the desert. Expert Egyptian builders built houses from bricks made of nothing but mud and chopped straw, baked hard in the sun.

⑥ The Egyptians were master craftspeople, builders and architects. Without the technology we have today, they built awe-inspiring temples and pyramids to worship their gods and their rulers. Abu Simbel is the site of two magnificent sandstone temples built by Pharaoh Ramses II, who reigned from 1279–1213 BCE. The entrances are guarded by statues of Ramses himself!

⑦ The Egyptian empire extended as far south as the kingdom of Kush, in modern-day Sudan, where the Egyptians encountered exotic animals like elephants and rhinos.

⑧ To journey up and down the Nile, the Egyptians built boats from plants called reeds.

⑨

Walking the 6,500-km length of the River Nile was the biggest adventure of my life. I saw strange ancient monuments looming out of the Egyptian desert and, fascinated, I began to explore, learning more about the incredible people who built these masterpieces. I discovered that humans used to be nomads who lived in tribes. This all started to change around 6000 BCE, when the burning sands of the Sahara Desert in Africa began to expand. The people who roamed its fringes were in danger of starving as the drought spread. The banks of the River Nile were rich and fertile – perfect for farming – so people travelled from all over Africa to settle there. As the population living on the riverbanks grew, people stopped hunting and gathering their food every day, and instead began to grow crops.

Settlers formed villages and towns, which eventually became ancient Egypt – the world's first proper civilisation, which lasted for almost 3,000 years. It was governed by rulers called pharaohs, who were worshipped as if they were gods. The Egyptians revered learning, and played a big part in creating one of the first forms of writing: hieroglyphs. I visited Luxor Temple, on the bank of the Nile, and marvelled at the ancient symbols carved into the walls – writing that is 3,500 years old!

This map shows the reach of the Egyptian empire about 3,500 years ago.

ALEXANDER THE GREAT
CONQUEROR OF THE WORLD

As I walked the vast deserts and plains of Arabia, I was treading in the footsteps of one of the greatest explorers, warriors and rulers the world has ever known. When Alexander the Great was born, in the ancient Greek kingdom of Macedon in 356 BCE, a temple burned. In those days, a burning temple prophesied a catastrophe. But no prophecy could have foreseen the impact this little baby would have on the world.

Alexander grew up in the court of his father, King Philip of Macedon. When he was 20 years old, Alexander's father was assassinated, and Alexander ascended the throne. Philip had been a great warrior, and the young king was determined to continue his legacy. He conquered all of Greece, then set his sights on the mighty Persian empire. With his army of Greek warriors, Alexander crossed into Asia Minor (what is now Turkey) and raged through Syria and Egypt, conquering everything in his path.

By the age of 25, Alexander had an impressive number of titles; he was king of Macedon, leader of the Greeks, overlord of Asia Minor, pharaoh of Egypt and great king of Persia. But still he remained unsatisfied. In the eight years that followed, Alexander and his army fought their way east, through Afghanistan all the way to what is now Pakistan and India.

Alexander was a mighty leader who fought in every battle and led from the front. He tamed a wild stallion, named Bucephalus, and rode him at the head of his army. But Alexander was also a great scholar, diplomat and explorer, who united his vast empire through trade. He explored the countries he captured – learning languages, immersing himself in new cultures and studying philosophy.

Alexander inspired huge loyalty in his troops, who followed him without question, but it must have been very hard for them to travel so far away from everything they knew. Though they might have been scared, my experiences have taught me that it is also an honour to push boundaries, cross new frontiers and visit remote and awesome places. To explore alongside Alexander must have been an incredible experience.

ALEXANDER'S EMPIRE

LOCATION MAP

Start

1 Alexander's epic journey began at Pella, the capital of Macedon, in 334 BCE.

PELLA

TROY

2 His army first did battle with the Persians near Troy.

3 The troops travelled on to Issus and again defeated the Persians, who were led by Emperor Darius III.

ISSUS

Mediterranean Sea

ARBELA

5 Alexander founded Alexandria in 332 BCE. It became the most important city in ancient Egypt.

7 At the Battle of Arbela in 331 BCE, Alexander defeated Darius III for good, conquering the Persian Empire.

ALEXANDRIA

Finish

GAZA

BABYLON

MEMPHIS

6 At Gaza, Alexander cheekily sent huge amounts of incense to his tutor at home, who had once told him off for wasting it.

EGYPT

4 Alexander was crowned pharaoh at Memphis in 332 BCE.

13 Alexander died at Babylon in 323 BCE. His body was taken to Alexandria, where it was placed in a golden coffin.

River Nile

Red Sea

ARABIA

PERSIA'S RULER

King Darius III was the emperor of Persia until Alexander overthrew him. The victors celebrated with a feast of Persian flavours they had never tasted before.

When I'm travelling, I'm often on the road for months at a time. It can be really tough – I miss my friends, my family and my own bed. But I count myself lucky I wasn't one of Alexander's soldiers – he and his army journeyed east for nine years! Battles were fought, empires fell and cities were ransacked before rising again from the ashes. I've always enjoyed returning home after an adventure, it's one of the best parts. But some of Alexander's troops were forced to settle in faraway lands to establish new towns. Alexander founded more than 70 cities, including Alexandria in Egypt and Kandahar in Afghanistan, and at its height his empire stretched across three continents, from Macedon in the west to India in the east, and as far south as Egypt. After travelling and fighting solidly for almost a decade, his exhausted army forced Alexander to turn back when they reached India. He died in Babylon in 323 BCE, possibly from poison or malaria.

9 Alexander ordered the assassination of one of his closest advisors at Ecbatana in 330 BCE.

ECBATANA

10 In 329 BCE, Alexander founded the city of Kandahar, in modern-day Afghanistan.

KANDAHAR

HYDASPES

8 Persepolis was the capital city of the Persian Empire. In 330 BCE, it was ransacked by Alexander.

PERSEPOLIS

PERSIA

11 At the Battle of Hydaspes, in what is now Afghanistan, Alexander's cavalry managed to defeat a force of 100 war elephants.

Arabian Sea

12 Alexander's war-weary troops forced him to head for home in 325 BCE.

THE SILK ROAD
A PRECIOUS JOURNEY BETWEEN WEST AND EAST

BYZANTIUM

Finish

ANATOLIA

8 ANTIOCH

NISHAPUR

CTESIPHON

SAMARKAND

DUNHUANG

PERSIA

ARABIA

AKSUM

INDIAN PENINSULA

Mediterranean Sea · Red Sea · Persian Gulf · Arabian Sea

7 Weary travellers feasted on delicacies such as figs, oranges, walnuts and wine at rest stops along the route.

6 Cities bordering the Silk Road grew rich from the money and trade passing through. Samarkand, in modern Uzbekistan, was one of the most important destinations on the Silk Road.

8 When the merchants finally reached the Mediterranean, ships carried the cargo over the waves to Italy to be distributed throughout Europe.

4 The high passes of the mighty Himalayan mountains were often blocked with ice and snow, and many travellers froze to death.

5 Rich Chinese merchants often wore their hair long, and donned ankle-length padded robes made of a sturdy and hard-wearing material called hemp.

14

3 Part of the Silk Road was protected by the Great Wall of China. Its ancient strongholds became wealthy as more and more merchants travelled along the route.

LOCATION MAP

Start

Yellow Sea

CHANGAN

2 Travellers along the trade route endured many dangers including animal attacks and ambushes from thieves and bandits.

CHINA

1 Prized throughout Asia and Europe for its softness and luxury, silk was a precious commodity. Only the Chinese knew how to make it, and so the Silk Road sprang into being.

South China Sea

Bay of Bengal

SOUTH-EAST ASIA

THE DIPLOMAT PRINCESS

The Silk Road didn't only play an important role in trade — it was also vital for diplomacy. Kingdoms in ancient China often forged relationships with their neighbours through marriage. So, Princess Wang Zhaojun of the Han travelled to marry a chieftain of the Hun people. She was an extremely talented diplomat, and the marriage was followed by decades of peace, trade and cultural exchanges. Her contribution to the smooth running of the Silk Road was so great that tradespeople from across political divides paid their respects when she died.

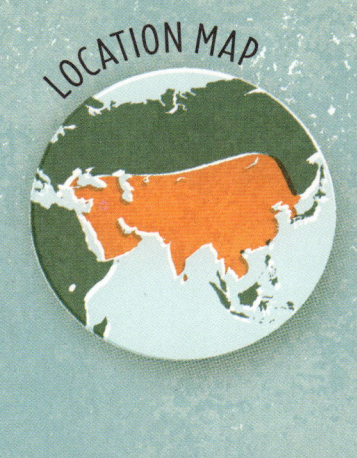

The phrase 'Silk Road' might conjure up for you a vast, dusty trail along which caravans of camels, horses and mules transported gems and silks. But the Silk Road wasn't really one road — it was a route made up of trails, bridges and pathways stretching for 8,000 km from the Pacific coast of China in the east to the Mediterranean Sea in the west. It is one of the most important trade routes the world has ever known. From the second century it helped to share ideas about commerce, culture and inventions across kingdoms and empires.

When I was 22 years old I travelled some of this route through Iran and Afghanistan, though — unlike the ancient travellers — I was lucky enough to journey by car, van and lorry instead of by camel or on foot. I was able to see the cities that were first made great by the passing wealth of the Silk traders, where old bazaars still stand and people have been trading for hundreds of years. The original explorers battled grave dangers, the scorching, barren deserts of Persia and the treacherous Himalayan mountains to sell their goods to the highest bidders in the markets of the west.

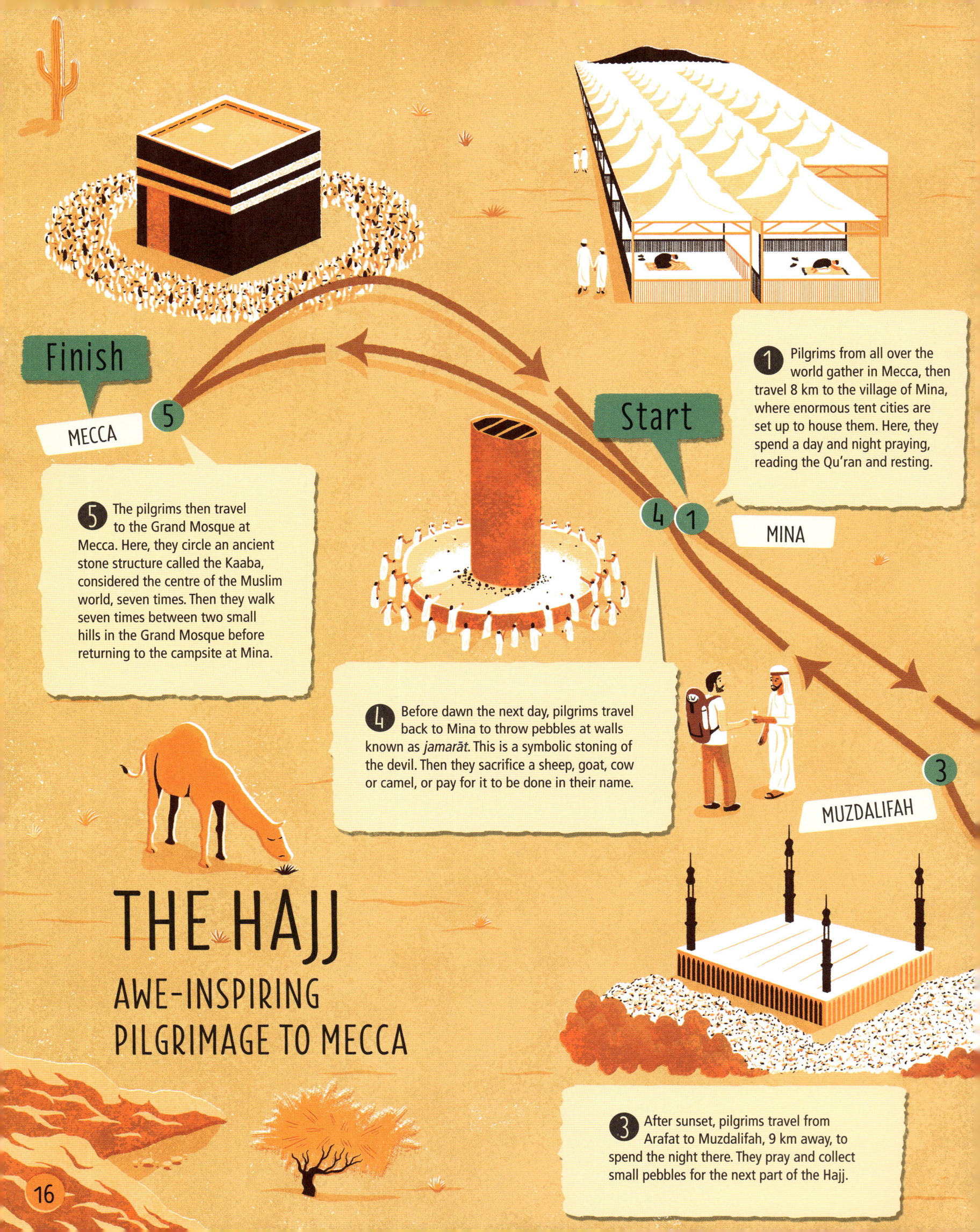

THE HAJJ
AWE-INSPIRING PILGRIMAGE TO MECCA

Finish — MECCA

Start — MINA

MUZDALIFAH

1 Pilgrims from all over the world gather in Mecca, then travel 8 km to the village of Mina, where enormous tent cities are set up to house them. Here, they spend a day and night praying, reading the Qu'ran and resting.

5 The pilgrims then travel to the Grand Mosque at Mecca. Here, they circle an ancient stone structure called the Kaaba, considered the centre of the Muslim world, seven times. Then they walk seven times between two small hills in the Grand Mosque before returning to the campsite at Mina.

4 Before dawn the next day, pilgrims travel back to Mina to throw pebbles at walls known as *jamarāt*. This is a symbolic stoning of the devil. Then they sacrifice a sheep, goat, cow or camel, or pay for it to be done in their name.

3 After sunset, pilgrims travel from Arafat to Muzdalifah, 9 km away, to spend the night there. They pray and collect small pebbles for the next part of the Hajj.

LOCATION MAP

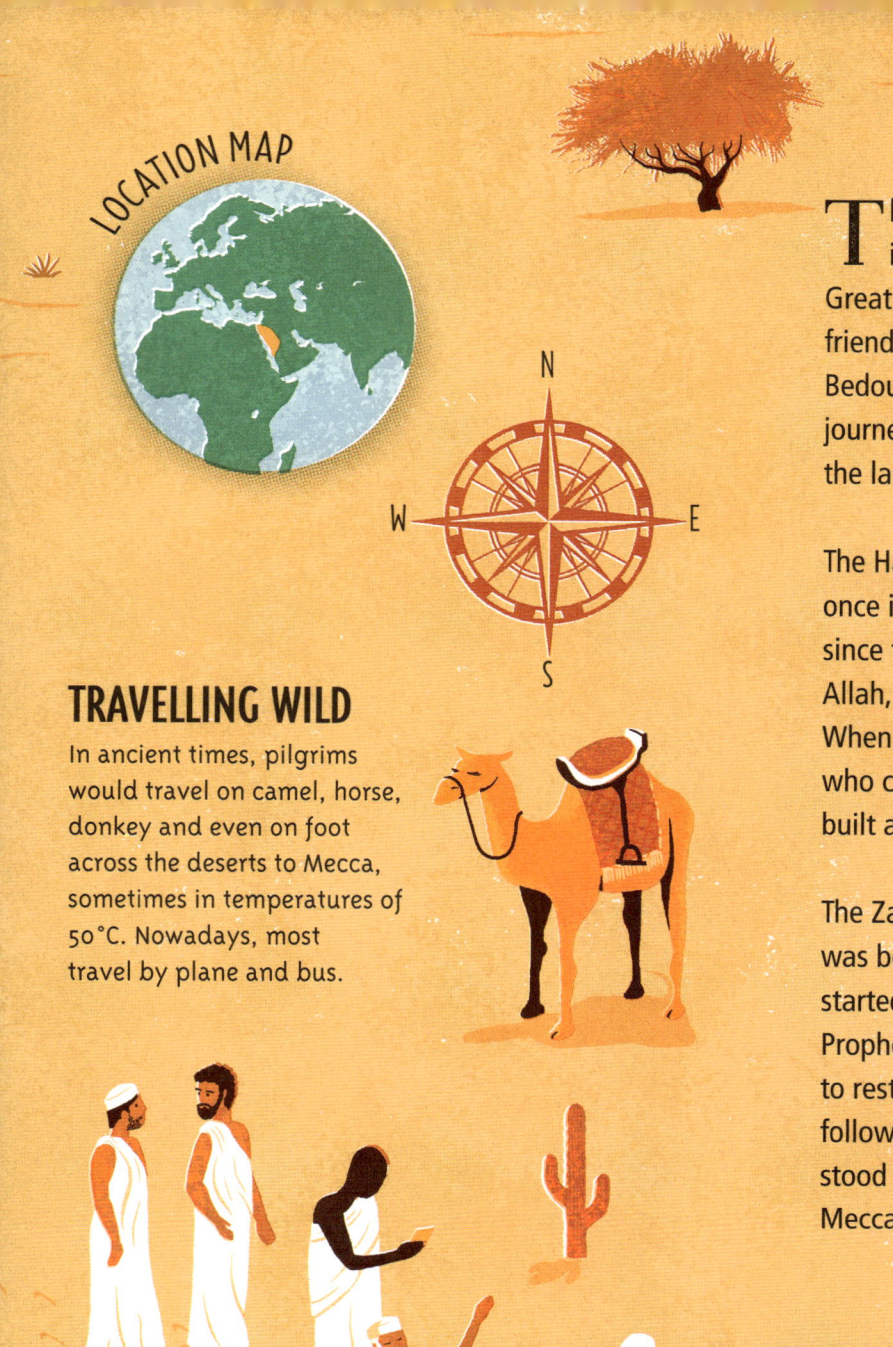

The immense, scorching deserts of Arabia have played host to intrepid explorers throughout the centuries, from Alexander the Great up to the present day. When I visited these lands, I found the friendliness of the people humbling. Everywhere I went, hospitable Bedouin nomads offered me tea and respite from my challenging journey. Every year, though, these incredible lands also welcome the largest annual gathering of humans on Earth: the Hajj.

The Hajj is a pilgrimage that every Muslim must carry out at least once in their lifetime if they are able to, and has been happening since the seventh century. Muslims believe it began when God, or Allah, told the Prophet Ibrahim to abandon his family in the desert. When they grew hungry and thirsty, Ibrahim's wife prayed to Allah, who created a spring of water, the Zam Zam, to save them. Ibrahim built a shrine at this site, which is now called the Kaaba.

The Zam Zam attracted trade and settlers, so a town called Mecca was born. It became a bustling metropolis, but the inhabitants started to worship other gods. So, in the seventh century, Allah sent Prophet Mohammed, the founder of Islam, on a pilgrimage to Mecca to restore it to the worship of Allah only. He set off with 1,400 followers on the first pilgrimage in Islamic history. This journey has stood the test of time – today, almost two million pilgrims travel to Mecca, in present-day Saudi Arabia, every year.

TRAVELLING WILD

In ancient times, pilgrims would travel on camel, horse, donkey and even on foot across the deserts to Mecca, sometimes in temperatures of 50°C. Nowadays, most travel by plane and bus.

RULES OF THE ROAD

Pilgrims follow rituals on their journey such as not shaving or cutting their nails, and not using scented soaps or perfumes. While on the Hajj, pilgrims are also not allowed to fight or argue, and must be very strict about how much food they eat.

To be pure for the journey, there are rules about clothing that all pilgrims must follow. Everyone should wear white, women cannot cover their face, even if it is the tradition in their home country, and men cannot have stitching on their clothes.

2 Next, the pilgrims travel 14.4 km to the Mount of Mercy at Arafat, the scene of the Prophet Mohammed's final sermon, to pray.

2 ARAFAT

Some of the most stunning places I've found have been in Sweden and Norway, the homelands of the Vikings. There are beautiful fjords, which are huge inlets carved out by slow-moving glaciers over hundreds of years. Visiting these dramatic landscapes steeped in history, it is not hard to see how they were the cradle of such a fearsome race of warriors, who raided and traded their way around the world for more than 300 years.

The Vikings came from modern-day Norway, Sweden and Denmark but sailed across the globe, seizing all the territory they could. Viking raiders made it to Germany, France, Spain, Italy, Ireland and Britain, and settled as far afield as Ukraine and Russia. They might even have reached Baghdad in modern-day Iraq! The Vikings weren't just ferocious fighters – they were great explorers too. A warrior called Leif Eriksson the Lucky even journeyed to the shores of North America.

Boats were essential to Viking culture. Their wooden longships were feats of engineering, designed to cover great distances. Longships had oars as well as sails in case there was no wind, and a shallow hull at one end so warriors could get off quickly to attack the enemy. Sea travel was at the centre of a Viking's life right up until their death. Some Vikings were even buried with their ships.

Viking clothes were made from wool, linen and animal skins. They spun wool into yarn, coloured it with natural plant dyes and wove it into tunics, trousers, dresses and pinafores.

Warriors stormed into battle in metal armour, carrying shields, wearing helmets and wielding ferocious axes and swords. Troops called berserkers would run ahead of raiding parties, shouting and screaming to scare the people they were attacking.

The Vikings ate quite a bland diet – oat porridge, salted meat, fish, fresh bread and lots of fruit. But they washed it all down with a strong alcoholic drink made from honey, called mead.

CONQUERORS OF THE SEA
THE VIKINGS

Vikings traded goods around the world. They took furs, tusks and seal fat south to warmer climates, and captured prisoners as slaves to sell in exchange for silver.

The Vikings weren't just ferocious fighters – they were great explorers too.

Vikings offered up animals or even people as sacrifices to their gods before a journey, to guarantee safe passage. Viking gods and goddesses included Odin, god of war, Thor, the god of thunder, and Freyja, the goddess of love and death, who rode a chariot pulled by two cats.

MARCO POLO
A LIFETIME OF ADVENTURE

Start

1 VENICE

1 At the time, Venice was part of the vast Holy Roman Empire, which stretched across Italy, France and Germany.

2 The Polos followed the Silk Road for four years, passing through Armenia, Azerbaijan and Persia, in modern-day Iran.

LOCATION MAP

3 While the expedition was walking through the mountains of central Asia, they named a type of sheep after Marco Polo!

AFRICA

ACRE

2

3

HORMUZ

ARABIA

PERSIA

Arabian Sea

20

When I hiked the Silk Road, I was also treading the path that another European adventurer had explored, hundreds of years before. Marco Polo was born in Venice in 1254, into a family of jewel merchants.

Marco's father and uncle were explorers, and returned from a lengthy expedition to the court of Kublai Khan, the emperor of China, when he was a teenager. Khan had sent the intrepid pair back with an order to bring him 100 missionaries to explain Christianity. Two years later, aged just 17, Marco Polo set off with his father and uncle to meet the Chinese emperor. He wouldn't see home again for more than 20 years, travelling all over Asia from India to China and even working for the emperor. When he eventually did return to Venice, he brought a taste of Asian culture to the western world.

5 Finally, the expedition reached Kublai Khan's palace at Xanadu (Shangdu, in modern-day China) where they were welcomed with open arms.

4 The travellers crossed the Gobi Desert on camels.

A FRIENDSHIP FILLED WITH RICHES

Marco Polo was in awe of Khan's empire, which sprawled across China and Mongolia. He enjoyed the local fermented horse milk drink, gazed in disbelief at a palace dining room that could seat 6,000 people and was astounded that Khan owned 10,000 horses! Polo and Khan became good friends, and Khan trusted him to serve as a diplomat and spy. He travelled to India and Burma, and even became the governor of Yangzhou in China. Khan died while Polo's expedition was returning home, cutting off all chances of the east-west route being passable for years to come.

6 Twenty years passed, Khan began to grow old, and his empire was in trouble following failed wars in Japan and Indonesia. Marco Polo decided it was time to go home. The journey back was full of danger – the travellers spent many months at sea and were robbed in Turkey – but eventually they reached Venice safely.

HOW TO BE AN EXPLORER

If uncovering the incredible stories of these explorers is starting to whet your appetite for adventure, then I'm thrilled! The whole wide world is out there, just waiting for you to go and discover it. But don't worry, your first trips don't have to be months-long expeditions. In fact, you can go on some incredible journeys just by stepping outside your front door! Just make sure you ask permission first. Here are my top tips for aspiring explorers…

START SMALL

Micro-adventures are a great way to start. When I was young, we lived on the edge of the Peak District in England, where we would go for weekend walks. And on one summer holiday, I remember hiking 5 km through the Scottish highlands. Start by going on walks in your local area, such as through a park or along a nearby river. Before you know it, you'll be ready to move on to national parks and wilderness areas.

BE ULTRA OBSERVANT!

When I get to the top of a steep hill, I make sure that I don't forget to turn around and enjoy the view! Take a camera or a sketch book to record what you see. I make sure to write a journal every night so I don't forget what happened – it comes in handy when I write my adventure books back home.

DISCOVER TALES OF ADVENTURE

I used to love the stories of bravery from the great polar explorers such as Scott and Shackleton. And other tales of Victorian exploration revealed the quest to reach the source of the Nile, which is what later inspired me to walk the great river's length from source to sea. Adventure travel books taught me about the character I'd need to have as an explorer.

BE CURIOUS

I have found adventure in the most unlikely places, often because of the fascinating people I have met. When I was 18, I saved up money to go travelling around the world on my own. I made friends with people from all walks of life and it made me even more curious about who else I could meet.

GET EQUIPPED!

When you're on an expedition, you're reliant on the team you have around you and your equipment. Take advice from people with experience on the best clothing and kit, and make sure you 'wear in' your boots before doing a long journey. A top traveller's tip is to wrap your feet in zinc oxide tape to stave off the blisters. I always take one smart white linen shirt too – it packs up small and light and means that I can be smart and presentable at the last minute if I need to. When I was in the Himalayas, it saved me from going to meet local dignitaries in a sweaty trekking t-shirt! But don't forget – you're going on an expedition, not a holiday, so pack light. I make sure I can comfortably carry all my kit in one backpack that I can walk with all day.

PITCH A TENT

I started camping in the garden at home. As I got older, I learnt how to pitch a tent myself – my family used to have competitions to see who could pitch theirs fastest. Tents are great if you want lots of protection from the elements. But on a recent trip to the Middle East, I didn't take a tent at all – it was warm enough to sleep in our sleeping bags under the stars! When it's a bit colder I use a bivvy bag – a cross between a sleeping bag and a one-person tent – which protects me from wind and rain.

LEARN HOW TO READ A MAP ...

In this day and age, it's very easy to become dependent on the GPS on our phones. I have to admit, I do use sat navs on expeditions – but it's important to learn how to read a map too in case of emergencies. When I was a boy I was in Cubs, which is part of the Scout Association, and that's where I was taught map-reading. We started indoors and were shown how to understand the key, contours, grid references and everything else. Once we'd got the hang of that, we put our new skills into practice racing to be the first back to checkpoints!

... AND A COMPASS

I did the Duke of Edinburgh Award when I was at school, which inspired me to go on adventures later on. We'd go on mini expeditions where we had to carry everything in our backpacks, including our tents and food – and most importantly, we had to navigate with a compass. When clouds roll in and there is low visibility, a compass can help you find your way to safety.

I've been on some lengthy trips in my time – walking through Central America took four months, trekking the Himalayas was a six-month journey and travelling the length of the Nile was an epic nine months! But this is really nothing compared to the adventures of a Muslim scholar named Ibn Battuta, which took him away from home for an astonishing 25 years!

In 1325, Ibn Battuta set out from his hometown of Tangier in Morocco, where he'd been born into a wealthy family of judges. He was going on the Hajj, the Islamic pilgrimage to Mecca, and he chose the least-used, longest route, which included following the Nile. It was a perilous journey – and trust me, I know all about it: crocodiles lurking in swamps and the fierce Egyptian sun are equally difficult beasts!

Ibn Battuta made it to Mecca in one piece, and his appetite for adventure was certainly whetted. He visited Africa and Asia, studying Islam in Damascus and Mecca, where he returned to complete the Hajj for a second time. During his third Hajj, Ibn Battuta heard about the Sultan of Delhi, a powerful ruler with a reputation for generosity. Ibn Battuta set out to visit him.

IBN BATTUTA
A 25-YEAR ODYSSEY

At first Ibn Battuta travelled with camel caravans – groups of camels and their handlers – along trade routes. Over time, he assembled his own team of servants and wives he met along the way. The group explored the great church of Hagia Sophia in Constantinople, the snow-covered steppes of Russia and the mountains of Afghanistan before crossing the treacherous Hindu Kush pass into India. Eventually they reached Delhi and were welcomed into the court. The sultan saw that Ibn Battuta was clever and hard-working, and appointed him a judge.

Ibn Battuta continued to travel though, and enjoyed writing about the strange animals that he encountered along the way, like rhinoceroses and hippopotamuses. In the Maldives he stayed just long enough to marry a princess, before carrying on east via Ceylon (modern-day Sri Lanka), finally reaching China in 1345. On arrival in the country he had to have his portrait painted for security reasons – a bit like a passport photo before cameras!

In 1346, Ibn Battuta decided to leave China and embark on the long journey home. He reached Morocco three years later, having been gone for almost 25 years. On his epic adventures, Ibn Battuta was beaten up by bandits, shipwrecked in storms, attacked by pirates and was married many times over. We know this because he wrote the stories of the 120,000 km he travelled in a book, showing us what life was like for an intrepid explorer in the fourteenth century.

> Ibn Battuta was beaten up by bandits, shipwrecked in storms, attacked by pirates and was married many times over.

7 The Hagia Sophia, in Constantinople (now Istanbul) was a church when Ibn Battuta travelled there. It later became a mosque, and now it's a museum.

3 Ibn Battuta was very impressed with the beauty of the Syrian city of Damascus. He described it as paradise, and stayed for 24 days.

1 Ibn Battuta's journey began in his home city of Tangier.

Black Sea

Caspian Sea

CONSTANTINOPLE

Start

Mediterranean Sea

TANGIER

TRIPOLI

DAMASCUS

BAGHDAD

2 At Tripoli, Ibn Battuta married the daughter of a government official.

CAIRO

Red Sea

MECCA

Ibn Battuta's journeys took him all over the world, from Africa to the Middle East and then on to Central and South Asia as far as China. He visited some of the world's most incredible cities, including Tripoli, Cairo, Jerusalem, Baghdad, Damascus, Djibouti, Kabul and Delhi! He travelled to the islands of the Maldives, Sumatra and Ceylon, which is now Sri Lanka. And what is really incredible is that he managed all of this with the most basic transport imaginable. He boarded sailing boats, rode a donkey, horse or camel, or sometimes even walked to travel about! Ibn Battuta and I have this in common. I've also travelled in all sorts of weird and wonderful ways, from lolloping about on yaks in the Himalayas, which feels like riding on a big sofa, to rickety boxes over the top of raging rivers, where you have to pull yourself across with a rope – making sure that you don't look down into the rapids below. It's definitely more exciting when you're not confined to a car or a plane!

TIMBUKTU

AFRICA

4 Ibn Battuta made the Hajj pilgrimage to Mecca three times.

MOGADISHU

6 Ibn Battuta described Kilwa as 'one of the most beautiful and well-constructed towns in the world'.

KILWA

26

IBN BATTUTA'S EPIC JOURNEY

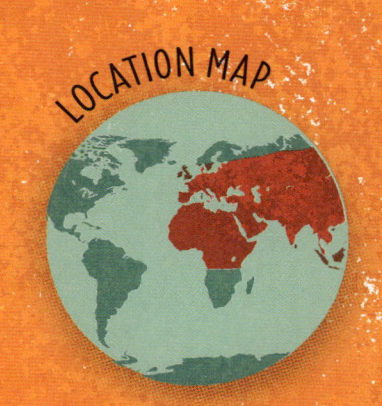

LOCATION MAP

8 In Delhi, the Sultan gave Ibn Battuta permission to live with a religious hermit in a cave for five months. Ibn Battuta got rid of all his possessions and took on the clothes of a beggar.

9 Ibn Battuta reached China in 1345. He admired how advanced the Chinese were – they were skilled at pottery, and everyone wore silk, even poor monks and beggars.

5 Ibn Battuta visited the ancient town of Baghdad in Iraq and marvelled at its glorious tiled bathhouses.

DELHI

CHINA — HANGZHOU

GUANGZHOU

East China Sea

SOUTH-EAST ASIA

South China Sea

Arabian Sea

INDIA

Bay of Bengal

CALICUT

CEYLON

Indian Ocean

KEY OF IBN'S TRAVELS
- 1325–1327
- 1327–1341
- 1341–1354

27

LOCATION MAP

9 At Aden, Zheng He bartered gold, silver, porcelain and pepper for rare gems, coral, amber and rosewater.

8 When he reached Hormuz, an island that is now part of Iran, Zheng He was convinced all the people there were very wealthy, because he saw no poverty, and traded riches such as sapphires, rubies, topaz, pearls, coral beads, amber, wool and beautiful carpets.

HORMUZ

ADEN

Indian Ocean

CALICUT

10 On Zheng He's later expeditions to the east coast of Africa, he traded gold, silver and silk from China for ostriches, zebras, camels, ivory and even a giraffe!

AFRICA

11 One of Zheng's fleet was shipwrecked off the coast of Kenya. Kenyan legend says that sailors who survived were granted permission to settle and marry there.

MADAGASCAR

Some of the journeys in this book are well known, and others are not. Zheng He's adventures were hardly known outside China until 2005, when the Chinese built 'Treasure Ship' park in the city of Nanjing in his honour. I was very excited to learn about his journeys around the world when the park opened.

Zheng He was named Ma Sanbao when he was born, around 1371 in the province of Yunnan, in present-day China. It was a place of jagged mountains and steep rice terraces, and at that time was ruled by the Mongol Empire. But when Ma Sanbao was 10, the Chinese tore into his town and captured him. He joined their army and grew up to be an officer skilled in diplomacy and war. He was also a tall and imposing man, said to be seven feet tall! He was chosen to be Commander-in-Chief for a new mission to explore the 'Western Oceans' and extend the influence of the Ming Empire. He was also awarded a new name – Zheng He – which was a great honour. In 1405, he set sail on his first naval journey. Over the next thirty years, Zheng He travelled to faraway lands, visiting Sri Lanka, Thailand, Indonesia, and even sailing as far as the western ports of India and the east coast of Africa.

ZHENG HE
THE UNKNOWN TRAVELLER

1 Zheng He's journey began at Nanjing, in China.

7 At Calicut, which is now in India, Zheng He encountered treachery from King Alagonakkara of Ceylon (now Sri Lanka), who had been pirating Chinese trade ships. Zheng He defeated and captured King Alagonakkara, and took him back to China where he forced him to apologise to the Emperor.

2 He became a hero in many Asian countries, and a bronze statue of him was unveiled in Quanzhou in 2005. Maritime Day, celebrated in China each year on 11 July, is dedicated to him.

CHINA

NANJING

QUANZHOU

VIETNAM

INDIA

CEYLON

QUY NHON

6 The Cakra Donya bell, a gift from Zheng He to the Indonesian town of Pasai, is now in a museum in Banda Aceh.

3 Quy Nhon, in modern-day Vietnam, was Zheng He's first foreign port of call on his epic voyages.

PASAI

BORNEO

PALEMBANG

5 At Palembang, Zheng He defeated and captured a ferocious pirate chief called Chen Zuyi.

4 At Surabaya, in present day Indonesia, is a mosque built by Chinese Indonesians, and named after Zheng He.

SURABAYA

CHRISTOPHER COLUMBUS
AND THE 'DISCOVERY' OF AMERICA

When I set out to write this book, I knew I wanted to include explorers whose discoveries had changed the world for ever. But that meant including people who had done harm as well as good – this next explorer is one example.

The adventurer Christopher Columbus was born in 1451 in Genoa, Italy. By the time he was in his thirties, he had sailed to Iceland, Ireland and the coast of West Africa. But he wanted to go further – to see what was on the other side of the Atlantic Ocean. He believed that if he travelled far enough he would reach India – at the time, nobody in Europe knew that America existed. Columbus was ambitious, fuelled by the desire for gold and the promise of adventure and glory. But he needed money to fund his expedition and won support from the king and queen of Spain, who were eager to expand their influence overseas.

His first expedition set sail from the Spanish port of Palos de la Frontera in 1492. Between then and 1504, Columbus completed four trips from Europe, across the Atlantic Ocean, to what was known then as the 'New World' but which today we call America. In that time, he planted the Spanish royal banner at San Salvador, in what is now the Bahamas, Hispaniola, now split into Haiti and the Dominican Republic, Venezuela, and many islands in the Caribbean. When Columbus headed for home, he took with him gold and parrots – not to mention the first potatoes, tomatoes, turkeys, pineapples, cocoa beans, tobacco and coffee beans ever seen in Europe. He was welcomed as a hero.

But it's important for us to consider what these events must have been like for the people living in the Americas. Their countries were invaded and their homes conquered by force. Until this point, the biggest animal in that part of the world was the llama, but Columbus and the armies that followed him cantered into villages and towns on horseback. People thought they were strange gods sent from the skies, and must have been terrified. The European invaders also carried diseases that they passed on to the people of the Americas, killing hundreds of thousands. In the century that followed Columbus's arrival in the Americas, millions of people died.

People sometimes refer to Columbus 'discovering' America, but actually there had been people living in the Americas for centuries, and vast established civilisations like the Maya lived there. It just so happened that, in 1451, Europeans were leaders in documenting the world's stories. This means we often hear the European version of history, rather than how it appeared to those who were invaded.

There is no denying, though, that by the time he died in 1506, Columbus had changed exploration, and the world, for ever – for better, and for worse.

When Columbus arrived home, he was welcomed as a hero.

MAGELLAN AND DRAKE

VOYAGES TO THE 'NEW WORLD'

When I was young, one of the most popular adventure stories around told of a seafaring explorer called Sir Francis Drake, who was so feared by his enemies that they called him The Dragon. He was said to have taken a snare drum all around the world on his journeys. Before he died he ordered it to be sent home to England, instructing that in times of trouble it should be beaten and he would return from the dead to save the nation. Now he is known in legend as the country's protector. This is his story.

In the sixteenth century there lived an Italian explorer called Amerigo Vespucci. He realised that the Caribbean islands Christopher Columbus had travelled to were part of a continent unknown to the Western world, meaning there was almost certainly more land beyond them to explore. The rulers of Spain asked a Portuguese man named Ferdinand Magellan to lead an expedition. In 1519, Magellan and his crew completed the first 'nearly complete' circumnavigation of the globe. They sailed to America, across the Pacific, around the Cape of Good Hope and back to Europe, disproving the popular theory that the Earth was flat. Tragically, Magellan didn't make it home – he was killed by a tribe in the Philippines.

Magellan disproved the popular theory that the Earth was flat.

In 1540, some 20 years after the death of Magellan, Francis Drake was born into a family of sea merchants and pirates in the southern town of Tavistock, in England. By the 1560s, he was commanding a ship between Africa and the Caribbean trading slaves – a cruel practice that involved capturing people in Africa and forcing them to work in the Caribbean. Drake's boat was attacked by the Spanish but he managed to escape and return home. It was a huge financial disaster, but it brought him to the attention of Queen Elizabeth I.

The queen wanted to compete with Spanish success, so in 1577 she gave Drake permission to see what lay beyond the Magellan Strait. The expedition sailed from Plymouth accompanied by supply ships so they wouldn't need to land in Spanish territory too often – which could lead to confrontations – and reached the coast of South America a few months later.

They crossed the Magellan Strait and then sped north, hugging the west coast of Chile. They raided Spanish towns and seized provisions along the way, and often chased and plundered Spanish ships – stealing gold, silver, pearls and other treasure. Drake claimed a strip of land in what is now California for Queen Elizabeth, and then sailed west towards the Philippines and eventually all the way around Africa. He returned to Plymouth with more than half of his crew still alive and plenty of treasure for Queen Elizabeth. She made him a knight and he became very rich and famous.

Drake's boat was attacked by the Spanish but he managed to escape!

THE ENDEAVOURS OF
CAPTAIN JAMES COOK

James Cook was born in Yorkshire, UK, in 1728. He was from a poor farming family, but in his teens he went to sea as a merchant apprentice and developed a fascination with ships. Cook worked furiously hard, studying maths and astronomy at night, before joining the navy and working his way up the ranks. When I was young I had ambitions to join the army, so I understand how hard Cook had to work to impress his seniors. Cook excelled and was the master of a ship before he was 30. He had already come a long way from his humble background, but his star was only just beginning to rise.

A decade passed, and the Royal Society, an organisation dedicated to research, decided to join forces with the navy on an expedition. Cook was appointed commander of the voyage, and given a ship named HMS *Endeavour*. She was bought by the navy specifically for the mission – she had spent the first four years of her life as a coal hauler. *Endeavour* weighed just 368 tonnes, which was small even for a sea-faring boat at the time. A container ship today usually weighs about 220,000 tonnes!

Officially, the expedition's aim was to observe the planet Venus from the island of Tahiti, but Cook had a secret mission too: to explore the mysterious waters between Asia and the Americas, and to try to find a large continent in the southern hemisphere which would 'balance out' all the land that had been discovered in the northern hemisphere. The cartographers who suspected this landmass existed called it *Terra Australis*. So with a crew of astronomers, artists and scientists on board, *Endeavour* sailed from Plymouth in August 1768.

In the Pacific islands, Cook came across tattoos for the first time. Many of the islanders would mark their skin extensively with traditional tribal body art. Sometimes they depicted Oro, also known as Mahui, the war god of Tahiti. He is said to enjoy fighting and demands human sacrifices during wartime, but becomes the god of peace in peacetime. Cook witnessed a human sacrifice to Oro while on Tahiti.

Cook returned to Britain in 1771. But the sea still called to him. His adventures weren't over yet ...

The intrepid expedition sailed on to New Zealand, then continued west to Australia. *Endeavour* was the first European ship to reach its east coast, landing at a natural harbour that Cook named Botany Bay. *Endeavour* nearly ran aground on the Great Barrier Reef, the world's largest coral reef that lurked beneath the waves, and Cook had to throw the ship's guns overboard to lighten the load and help the boat to move again. Further danger awaited the travellers when they were struck by a fever, claiming the lives of 30 expedition members.

The survivors set a course for home, travelling via Jakarta in Indonesia and the Cape of Good Hope in South Africa. Cook returned to Britain in July 1771 having circumnavigated the globe. Famous throughout the land, he even met the king! But the sea still called to him. Cook's adventures weren't over yet…

COOK'S VOYAGES

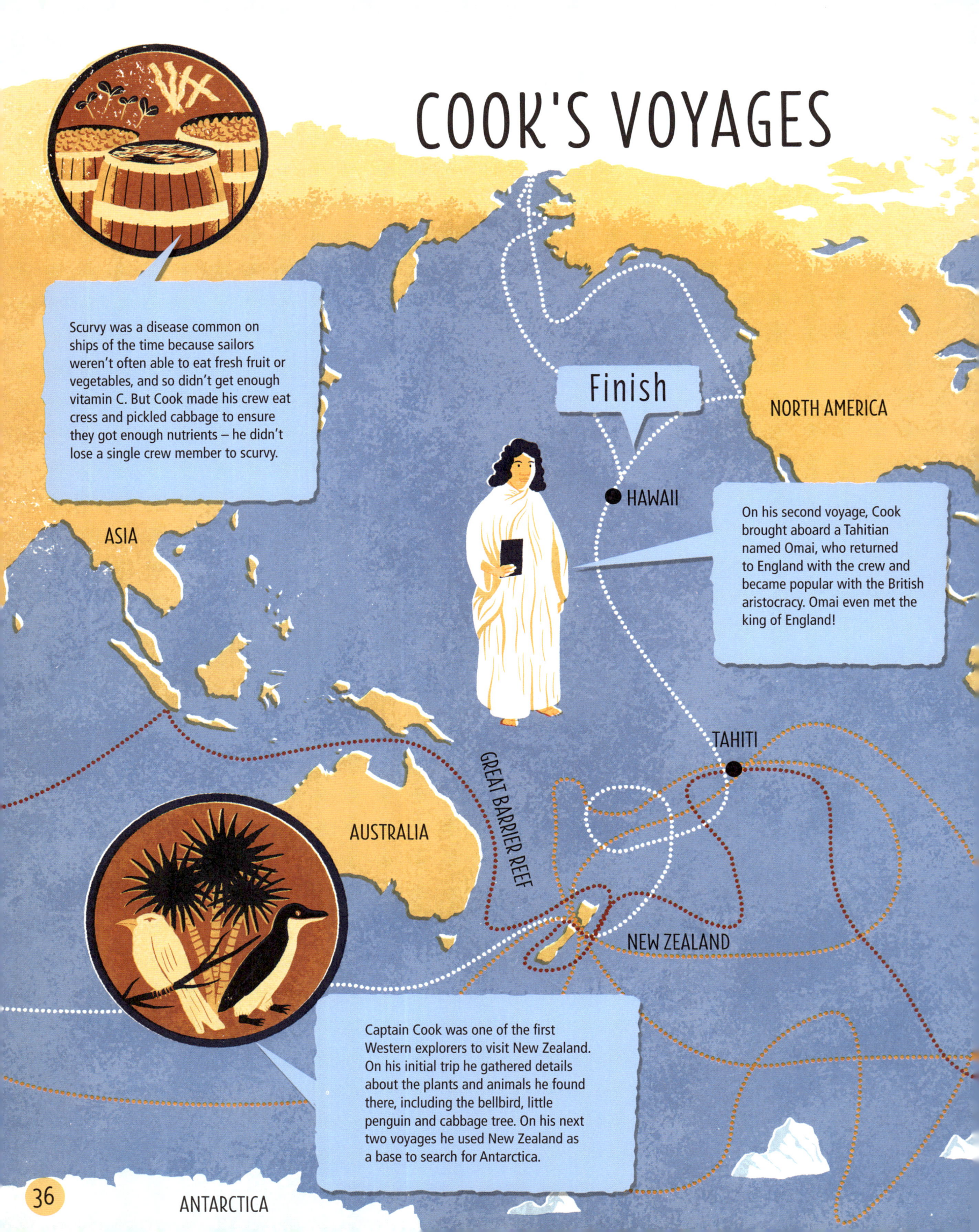

Scurvy was a disease common on ships of the time because sailors weren't often able to eat fresh fruit or vegetables, and so didn't get enough vitamin C. But Cook made his crew eat cress and pickled cabbage to ensure they got enough nutrients – he didn't lose a single crew member to scurvy.

Finish

NORTH AMERICA

HAWAII

On his second voyage, Cook brought aboard a Tahitian named Omai, who returned to England with the crew and became popular with the British aristocracy. Omai even met the king of England!

ASIA

TAHITI

GREAT BARRIER REEF

AUSTRALIA

NEW ZEALAND

Captain Cook was one of the first Western explorers to visit New Zealand. On his initial trip he gathered details about the plants and animals he found there, including the bellbird, little penguin and cabbage tree. On his next two voyages he used New Zealand as a base to search for Antarctica.

ANTARCTICA

A chronometer is a clock that can function in spite of the motion of a ship and a variation in temperature. This was necessary for Cook's expeditions, because they travelled between very hot places like Africa and very cold places such as Antarctica.

THE ARCTIC

Start

PLYMOUTH

EUROPE

In 1772, Cook set sail in the HMS *Resolution* and headed south. He even entered the Antarctic Circle before being forced to turn back by ice, storms and the extreme cold.

Cook could have retired rich, but he still sought out a northwest passage linking the Pacific and Atlantic. He set off in 1776, but, unable to discover a route, the expedition landed on Hawaii. The islanders were very friendly, but a row broke out when they stole one of Cook's boats. He was stabbed to death when he tried to recover it.

It was a tragic end for a great captain, but his three daring voyages ensured his legacy as an incredible exploring pioneer.

KEY
FIRST VOYAGE: 1768–1771
SECOND VOYAGE: 1772–1775
THIRD VOYAGE: 1776–1779

AFRICA

SOUTH AMERICA

On 17 January 1773, HMS *Resolution* was the first recorded vessel to cross the Antarctic Circle, but was not able to travel further south due to bad weather and icebergs.

BRITISH NORTH AMERICA (CANADA)

LOCATION MAP

Ocean in view! O! The joy.

UNCLAIMED TERRITORY

Columbia river

BEAVERHEAD ROCK

CAMP FORTUNATE

SPANIDISH TERRITORY

4 When the expedition reached Beaverhead Rock, a Shoshone landmark, they came across a group of 60 long-haired warriors mounted on horses, who were all members of the Shoshone tribe.

5 When Lewis and Clark met the Shoshone, they were in desperate need of horses to continue the journey, so they asked to negotiate with the chief. As he arrived, Sacagawea embraced him — he was her brother. Lewis and Clark named the site 'Camp Fortunate' to celebrate this luck.

6 The route was very mountainous, and at one point the expedition climbed a ridge, hoping to glimpse the Pacific Ocean, but was disappointed to see even more steep hills and valleys.

7 They were led by a Shoshone guide called Old Toby. It was a long, cold, miserable trek and they nearly starved, but they were saved by Old Toby, and his knowledge of the local wilderness. The expedition finally sighted the Pacific Ocean on 7 November 1805.

8 Lewis and Clark held a vote about where they should spend the winter before starting the long journey home. They included a slave named York and Sacagawea in the vote, which was unusual at the time as slaves and women did not have the right to vote.

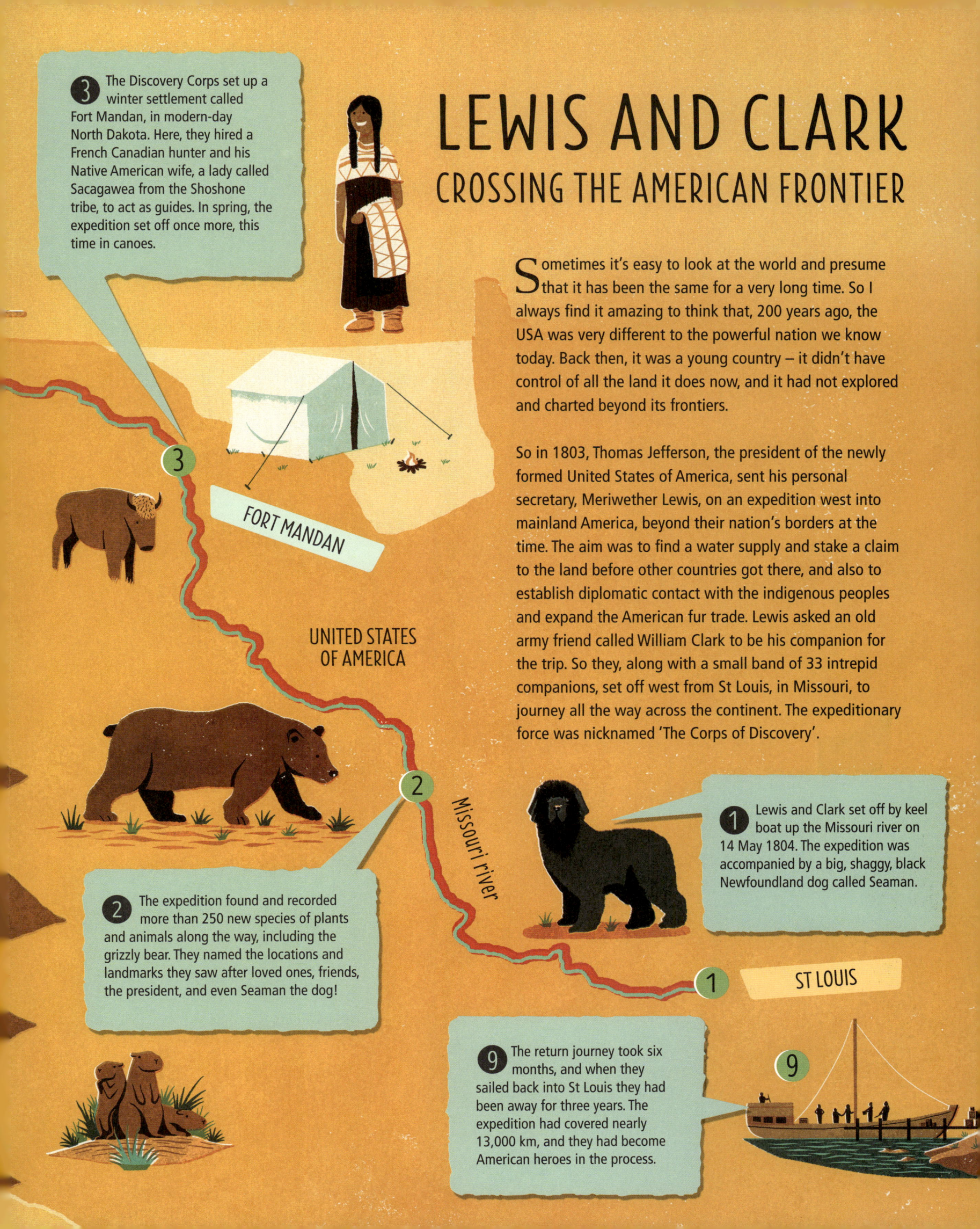

LEWIS AND CLARK
CROSSING THE AMERICAN FRONTIER

3 The Discovery Corps set up a winter settlement called Fort Mandan, in modern-day North Dakota. Here, they hired a French Canadian hunter and his Native American wife, a lady called Sacagawea from the Shoshone tribe, to act as guides. In spring, the expedition set off once more, this time in canoes.

Sometimes it's easy to look at the world and presume that it has been the same for a very long time. So I always find it amazing to think that, 200 years ago, the USA was very different to the powerful nation we know today. Back then, it was a young country – it didn't have control of all the land it does now, and it had not explored and charted beyond its frontiers.

So in 1803, Thomas Jefferson, the president of the newly formed United States of America, sent his personal secretary, Meriwether Lewis, on an expedition west into mainland America, beyond their nation's borders at the time. The aim was to find a water supply and stake a claim to the land before other countries got there, and also to establish diplomatic contact with the indigenous peoples and expand the American fur trade. Lewis asked an old army friend called William Clark to be his companion for the trip. So they, along with a small band of 33 intrepid companions, set off west from St Louis, in Missouri, to journey all the way across the continent. The expeditionary force was nicknamed 'The Corps of Discovery'.

FORT MANDAN

UNITED STATES OF AMERICA

Missouri river

1 Lewis and Clark set off by keel boat up the Missouri river on 14 May 1804. The expedition was accompanied by a big, shaggy, black Newfoundland dog called Seaman.

2 The expedition found and recorded more than 250 new species of plants and animals along the way, including the grizzly bear. They named the locations and landmarks they saw after loved ones, friends, the president, and even Seaman the dog!

ST LOUIS

9 The return journey took six months, and when they sailed back into St Louis they had been away for three years. The expedition had covered nearly 13,000 km, and they had become American heroes in the process.

THE EVOLUTION OF SCIENCE
CHARLES DARWIN

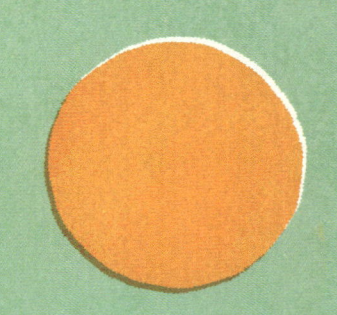

There is a strong link between exploration and scientific discovery. On journeys to new and exciting places, we can push boundaries and find out new things – both about ourselves (I've learned a great deal about what I'm capable of!) and about the world around us. In the nineteenth century, journeys to sea were a huge part of scientific discovery about flora, fauna and geology. Few would be more important, or ground-breaking, than the naturalist Charles Darwin's voyage on HMS *Beagle*.

In 1831, at the age of 22, Darwin joined the *Beagle* on its journey to South America. The expedition had many purposes: to survey the land and ocean along the route and to draw up maps and promote British trade. The five-year voyage made young Darwin seasick. I got ill on a dhow in the Gulf of Aden recently, and I can attest to how unpleasant it is. But the trip was worth it because it gave Darwin ample opportunity to explore the wilderness of South America, where the naturalist discovered fossils, observed animals and met tribespeople.

> For Darwin, there was no exciting discovery of a new land, but a slow development of scientific ideas brewing in his curious mind.

In the Andean mountains in Chile, Darwin felt an earthquake and witnessed a volcanic eruption, but he was more interested in the mussel beds along a neighbouring shore. These sat above the high tideline, so Darwin realised the mountains were being pushed up by seismic shifts in the Earth's crust.

Later, on a beach in Brazil, he found bones too big to belong to any known living animal, and concluded that the creatures must have died out. Journeying on, the expedition called at the lusciously fertile Galápagos Islands, where Darwin avidly noted down rare bird species and giant tortoises. He constantly searched for explanations about the history of Earth.

For Charles Darwin, there was no great conquering moment or exciting discovery of a new land, but a slow development of scientific ideas brewing in his curious mind. He returned from his voyage with lots of questions that he spent a lifetime trying to answer.

After years of experiments and hard work, Darwin published *On The Origin of the Species* in 1859, which proposed the theory that humans evolved from apes. The book was extremely controversial because it undermined the creation story central to Christianity, but it changed the course of history forever.

TRAILBLAZERS

In the pages of this book you'll find countless stories of daring and adventure, of people who set out to achieve something for the very first time. But the truth is, there are hundreds more explorers who inspire me every day, and I want to introduce you to as many of them as possible. Here are some of the others who have blazed a trail, going further than anyone believed they could.

ESTEBAN DE DORANTES

Esteban de Dorantes was an enslaved Moroccan who was one of the first indigenous Africans to reach what is now the USA, in the year 1527. The ship he was on was wrecked off the coast of the south-west USA, and he and a few other survivors went on to explore deserts and jungles towards what would become Mexico. Esteban's enviable skills as a talented linguist helped him to interact with all the indigenous people he met along the way.

JEANNE BARET

Jeanne Baret was a talented botanist who was born in 1740. She soon grew curious about all of the unknown flora still to be discovered around the world, so she disguised herself as a man and boarded a ship bound for the Americas. Without realising it, she became the first woman to circumnavigate the world! Along the way, she documented many little-known plants. When I set off to walk the length of the River Nile, I expected it to take anything between six and 24 months. It ended up taking nine, which was more than enough time to make me miss the comforts of home – but it's estimated that Baret was away at sea for three years!

ERIK WEIHENMAYER

Erik Weihenmayer was always a talented climber, and going blind as a teenager didn't deter him. He summited North America's highest point, Mount Denali, in his twenties. By 2001 he became the first blind person to summit Mount Everest – and by 2008 he'd climbed the highest peaks on all seven continents. I've climbed in the Himalayas and it's enormously challenging; there are so many things that can go wrong and I rely heavily on my sight to look for footholds and emergency escape routes. The skill and fortitude required to complete such a demanding journey without the help of your eyes is a monumental achievement.

GUDRIDUR THORBJARNARDOTTIR

Born in Iceland around 980, the Norse explorer Gudridur Thorbjarnardottir set off on a voyage to Greenland with her father when she was just a teenager. Naturally adventurous, she journeyed on to Viking leader Leif Erikson's settlement in America, making her one of the first women explorers. Some Viking women went on raiding and trading expeditions and could have relatively powerful positions in society but, even by Viking standards, Gudridur made some epic journeys across the world.

VALENTINA TERESHKOVA

Valentina Tereshkova was born in rural Russia and soon became obsessed with sky diving. But she worked in a factory and only parachuted in her spare time, so flying into the atmosphere seemed like an impossibility. In 1961, she heard about an opportunity to become the first woman to go into space, and she volunteered without hesitation. After rigorous training she flew into the sky in a tiny spaceship called *Vostok 6*. She was only 26 and totally alone, but in less than three days she managed to orbit Earth 48 times. She's still the only woman to have undertaken a solo mission in space.

LOCATION MAP

UGANDA

6 Speke carried on without his companion and, in the summer of 1858, he set eyes on another vast expanse of water, which he named Lake Victoria in honour of his queen. Speke had gone temporarily blind due to an illness, but he felt sure that he had found the source of the Nile.

DEMOCRATIC REPUBLIC OF CONGO

RWANDA

Lake Victoria

BURUNDI

TANZANIA

4 The duo were the first Europeans to reach the shores of Lake Tanganyika, the world's longest freshwater lake. But Burton was now very sick, and Speke explored the northern part of the lake in a canoe alone.

5 With Burton's health still failing, they decided to retrace their steps to Kazeh.

KAZEH

Lake Tanganyika

MEETING THE BAKERS

On his next expedition along the course of the Nile, Speke found the tributary from Lake Victoria that led to the Nile, proving him right. He also met an exploring party led by Samuel Baker and his future wife, Florence, who were looking for the river's source too. They were sad to learn that it had already been found, but later discovered another enormous body of water, Lake Albert, which also flowed into the Nile.

3 Along the way, the two men fell seriously ill from tropical diseases and suffered from hallucinations – Speke even made himself temporarily deaf by trying to dig a beetle out of his ear with a knife.

44

BURTON, SPEKE AND BAKER
SEARCH FOR THE SOURCE OF THE NILE

In 2013, one of my incredible journeys was walking the length of the River Nile, one of the longest rivers in the world. It took me an epic nine months, but I was following in the footsteps of my hero Richard Francis Burton, who was a soldier in the British Army when Queen Victoria was on the throne. He was a formidable and fearless man who loved to travel and learned more than 40 languages. His greatest obsession was to find the source of the Nile. The mystery had gripped explorers since an Egyptian expedition 2,000 years earlier had discovered that the Blue Nile began in Ethiopia. But the source of the White Nile – the main river – was unknown, because travelling its length was virtually impossible thanks to its many dangerous waterfalls and rapids. So in 1857, Burton and another explorer, John Hanning Speke, set off on a daring mission to Africa to discover the Nile's source by working towards the river from the east, rather than following its mighty path.

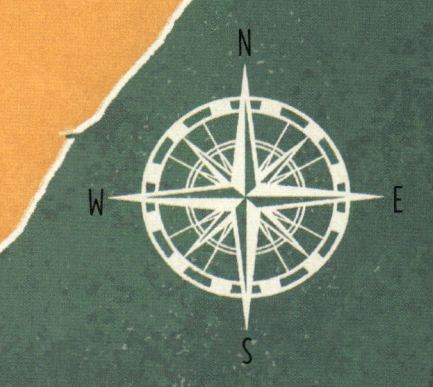

SOMALIA

KENYA

Indian Ocean

1 From the island of Zanzibar, Burton and Speke set off with an expedition team of over 50 people, including African porters, slaves, and Baluchi soldiers to protect them. Disorder broke out as soon as they set off – supplies were stolen, people deserted and there was even a mutiny among the soldiers!

ZANZIBAR

2 Travelling inland on foot and by donkey, progress was slow. They trekked through swamps and jungles using machetes to cut a path for themselves.

45

LIVINGSTONE, STANLEY & KINGSLEY
THE HEART OF AFRICA

The interior of Africa has long been a source of fascination for explorers, and I am no exception. The stories of epic adventures among the countless rivers, mountains and jungles of this astonishing continent inspired me to go on my own expedition through the heart of Africa.

That was only one trip of many for me, but Scottish missionary David Livingstone made charting Africa his life's work, alongside ceaselessly trying to bring an end to slavery by encouraging trade of legitimate goods between Africans and Europeans. Livingstone spent many years travelling in Africa, often accompanied by his wife Mary, going further than any other European had been before. He learned the languages and observed the customs of the local people. It was dangerous work – he was once mauled by a lion – but Livingstone was defiant, saying, 'I shall open up a path into the interior, or perish.' Perhaps his greatest success was becoming the first European to see the magnificent waterfalls on the Zambezi river on the border of Zambia and Zimbabwe. In 1866, Livingstone set off in search of the source of the Nile, hoping that if he found it and became famous, he might be able to use his influence to stop the terrible trade in humans.

In 1871, an adventurous journalist named Henry Morton Stanley was sent to Africa by the *New York Herald* to search for Livingstone, who hadn't been heard from for some years. When he eventually found him, he greeted the sick man with the famous words, 'Dr Livingstone, I presume?' Livingstone died two years later from malaria. His body was returned to Britain and buried in London's Westminster Abbey, but his heart was buried in Africa, the continent he loved so dearly.

"Dr Livingstone, I presume?"

After Livingstone's death, Stanley became determined to take up his hero's mantel and continue exploring Africa. He went on to travel across vast areas, and made an epic 4,700-km journey along the entire Congo river. He also won financial support from the king of Belgium to develop the region and to start building roads.

Two decades later, in 1893, another writer followed in Stanley's footsteps. Mary Kingsley had inherited a large amount of money and outraged polite society by spending it on a one-way ticket to Africa. She had many adventures, often going canoeing to study the local wildlife, which involved carefully avoiding a hippo trap! In doing so, Kingsley discovered four species of freshwater fish. She also trekked through the jungle for kilometres with a broken ankle, and became the first European to reach Gabon, on the west coast of Africa. She returned to London a heroine because her courage proved that women could also be explorers. The books she wrote about her expedition showed a real insight into the cultures of central Africa, and helped to change British attitudes towards the continent and its people.

AROUND THE WORLD WITH NELLIE BLY

Nellie Bly was a pioneering journalist from Pennsylvania, USA. She was born Elizabeth Cochran in 1864 – but when she started working as a journalist, she adopted the pen name Nellie Bly after a famous song of the day.

Her writing career began when she read an article in a local newspaper that said women should stay at home rather than go to work. Bly felt this was not acceptable. She wrote such a fierce and thoughtful response to it that the editor of the paper gave her a job. As a journalist she was dedicated to telling honest stories and making voices heard. She would go undercover and take on a disguise in order to expose the truth about psychiatric hospitals or factory conditions for women. Not only did this force these places to reform their ways, but it won her fame and acclaim as a great reporter and gave her the opportunity to go on exciting adventures.

Bly's most ambitious and treacherous journey was in 1889 when she decided to travel around the world for a newspaper report. She wanted to test the fictional challenge in *Around the World in Eighty Days*, a novel by Jules Verne in which the lead character, Phineas Fogg, circumnavigates the globe in 80 days.

Bly set a world record and became an international star!

Bly was only 25 when she set off from New Jersey, USA and travelled by boat to the UK for her first leg. Like me, she travelled light, wearing a sturdy overcoat to keep out the cold and carrying a small travel bag with a change of underwear. From Britain she crossed into France, where she went to meet Jules Verne, the author who had inspired her brave adventure. He wished her luck and off she set to tackle the rest of her expedition.

It's hard to imagine in our times of instant communication, but Bly's updates were sent by telegraph and by post, taking weeks to arrive. So her progress was a mystery most of the time, but as soon as news did arrive, the *World* newspaper would breathlessly make its reports. Its readers were gripped by her journey and the paper ran a competition to guess how long Bly would take. Undeterred by the high expectations, she fearlessly crossed Italy, Egypt, Sri Lanka, Singapore, Hong Kong and Japan. Bly travelled by rickshaw, railway, bus, horse and even a sampan, which is a small flat-bottomed Asian boat. When I circumnavigated the Arabian peninsula, I used lots of different methods of transport too, including donkey, camel, hitch-hiking, dhow and even a tank. I've learnt that when you travel the way the locals do, you're forced to slow down and get to meet some amazing people. But Bly was in more of a rush — she had an imaginary record to beat!

From Japan she boarded another ship to cross the Pacific back to the USA. She arrived in San Francisco and had to race west across the country to get back to New Jersey. Only 72 days after she had left, Bly was greeted back in New York with fireworks. She'd set a world record and her journey had made her an international star.

49

TO THE POLES
FEATS OF ENDURANCE

By the beginning of the twentieth century, most places on the planet had been explored. But one of the most challenging regions remained untouched: the poles. I've been to the coldest inhabited place on Earth: Oymakon in eastern Siberia, just outside the Arctic Circle. I've seen first-hand that if you throw boiling water into the sky, it turns into snow immediately.

A century before I visited, an American naval officer named Robert Peary and his African American field assistant, Matthew Henson, led a number of expeditions to the Arctic. In 1909, Peary and Henson's team were announced as the first to reach the North Pole, although there has since been some dispute. Either way, they returned home as heroes. Peary went on to become president of the Explorers Club, and in 1937, Henson was the first African American person to be made an honorary member of the club.

With the North Pole explored, in 1911 a competitive race began to reach the South. The main contenders were Norwegian Roald Amundsen and the Briton Robert Falcon Scott. Amundsen's starting point was almost 100 km closer to the pole than Scott's, and that wasn't the only difference – his team used skis rather than sleds. After weeks trekking across ice and snow and nights freezing in a draughty tent, Amundsen and his team reached the South Pole first. He planted a Norwegian flag in the ground so when, a few weeks later, Scott and his team reached the South Pole, they were devastated to find out they had been beaten. They set off back to their ship but were caught in a blizzard just a few kilometres from safety. Sadly, they all perished from cold and starvation.

Endurance was crushed by the pressure of shifting ice.

Scott had made an earlier expedition to Antarctica, and on that ship was a man named Ernest Shackleton. He had been knighted for his exploits with Scott, and Shackleton was eager to explore Antarctica further. His ship was called *Endurance*, after his family motto, 'By endurance we conquer'. *Endurance* set sail from South Georgia on 5 December 1914.

The ship battled through 1,000 km of ice, but on 19 January 1915, true disaster struck: *Endurance* became trapped. The crew were forced to camp on the ice while they waited for spring to arrive, even building igloos for their dogs and calling the settlement Dogtown. We know what life in the camp was like because the expedition had a photographer called Frank Hurley. He was so committed that he once dived into freezing water to save his photograph slides. That's dedication!

When spring finally arrived, it didn't set the ship free as the crew had hoped. Instead, on 27 October, *Endurance* was crushed by the pressure of shifting ice. The lifeboats were quickly salvaged, and then she sank. Shackleton and his crew trekked off in search of safer ice. Morale was starting to fade, but one day the camp was attacked by a leopard seal. Upon shooting it, the team were delighted to find the seal's stomach filled with undigested fish that they could eat. Six months later, the intrepid crew squeezed into three lifeboats and set off for uninhabited Elephant Island. Though they arrived safely, Shackleton knew they had no chance of being rescued from there. So, exhausted and weary, he set sail with five crew once more – this time on a desperate, 1,300-km voyage across the ocean to South Georgia. Incredibly, they made it – and when they returned four months later with a rescue party, they found the rest of the crew alive too. Somehow, Shackleton had managed to survive the ordeal without losing a single team member.

ISABELLA BIRD

Some adventurers look forward to the creature comforts of home when they return after a long journey. That was *not* the case for Isabella Bird, who, once she started exploring aged 40, rarely managed to stay at home for a few months before setting off again. 'I abhor civilisation!' she once exclaimed. Perhaps her most celebrated journey was through the Persian Gulf, where she hiked and travelled by mule in freezing temperatures, surviving blizzards, robberies and intense hunger. I am always amazed by her strength – ever since childhood Bird had suffered from back problems, but she always ploughed on and never let her health stop her from going on adventures. In fact, she first started adventuring outdoors to try and improve her constitution!

WOMEN IN THE MIDDLE EAST

I recently circumnavigated the Arabian peninsula and can confirm that this oblong-shaped landmass is home to some of the most challenging deserts and hostile environments on Earth! It was even more difficult to travel there 150 years ago, but that never stopped the incredible women who have explored the sands of Arabia. Here are just a few of my favourites...

FREYA STARK

For the intrepid adventurer Freya Stark, travelling was all about stories – she picked the Middle East for her first trip because her favourite childhood book was *The Arabian Nights*. Stark would plod along on the back of a mule in the hot desert sun in search of villages and landmarks in the Middle East that she'd heard of, and was often the first European woman the local people had ever seen. Despite catching malaria and dengue fever, she always kept going. In 1931, she visited the Valley of Assassins, home to a dangerous Persian tribe known for murdering visitors – but thankfully, she survived.

GERTRUDE BELL

Gertrude Bell learned to climb mountains in the Alps, but her lifelong fascination was with the Middle East. In 1892, she set off through Iraq, Syria and Iran recording her observations and experiences. She led archaeological digs in Iraq and wrote the country's first antiquities law. When the First World War broke out, she became a diplomat and spy, utilising her knowledge of local languages and her regional contacts to become indispensable.

DERVLA MURPHY

Murphy set off on a bicycle in 1963, determined to travel solo from her homeland in Ireland across Europe and the Middle East to reach India. She did it – and along the way she fractured three ribs in Afghanistan, and even stayed with a *wali*, or Islamic saint, in Pakistan. She's been travelling ever since, to Peru and Siberia, Ethiopia and Jordan, writing books about her adventures as she goes. In recent years she's explored life in Israel and Palestine, seeking to understand the tensions found across the divide.

JANE DIEULAFOY

Dieulafoy was a French woman who was determined not to let society's expectations hold her back. When her husband Marcel was sent to the front of the Franco-Prussian war, she made sure she wasn't left behind. Disguised in a soldier's uniform, she fought for her country by his side. It was a habit that stuck – during her later adventures abroad, Dieulafoy wore men's clothing and cut her hair short. She and Marcel went to Persia in 1881 to take part in an archaeological dig at Susa. To get there, they had to trek 6,000 km on horseback. When eight bandits tried to accost her, Dieulafoy held them off at gunpoint, telling them, 'I have 14 balls of gunpowder at my disposal. Come back with six more friends.'

AMELIA EARHART
A WOMAN WITHOUT LIMITS

Whenever I think of someone pushing boundaries and challenging conventions, I think of Amelia Earhart. Her epic journeys mark her out as one of the most daring people who has ever lived.

'By the time I had got two or three hundred feet off the ground, I knew I had to fly.'

Earhart was born in Kansas in 1897 and loved playing outside and climbing trees. She once even built a rollercoaster in her back garden! But it was a day out at a stunt-flying exhibition almost a decade later that sealed her destiny. A pilot in a plane spotted Earhart and her friend watching and decided to give them a scare, diving straight at them. But gutsy Earhart refused to budge. 'I believe that little red airplane said something to me as it swished by,' she later reflected. In 1920, she finally sat as a passenger in a plane. 'By the time I had got two or three hundred feet off the ground, I knew I had to fly,' she later said.

She was so determined to learn that she tracked down one of the best aviators of the day, Neta Snook, and begged her for lessons. The airfield was a long way from home, and she had to take a long bus to the final stop and then walk for over 6 km, but Earhart wouldn't let a little thing like that stop her. And sure enough, after just a couple of years, she owned a plane and had her pilot's licence. She was only the sixteenth woman in the USA to be issued with a licence.

She nicknamed that first plane, a bright yellow biplane, 'The Canary', and immediately got to work setting records, becoming the first woman to rise to an altitude of 14,000 feet (4,267 m). It wasn't long before she became a celebrity, earning the moniker the Queen of the Air.

In 1932 she embarked on her longest journey yet — flying solo across the Atlantic. Many people had tried and died in the attempt, and only one other person — Charles Lindbergh — had achieved it before. She took off from Newfoundland on the east coast of Canada, alone, in a tiny single-engine wooden plane she called her 'Little Red Bus'. When I was in the British Army I was in the Parachute Regiment, the airborne specialists, and I spent a lot of time in planes in dangerous conditions. But I always had my team of fellow soldiers alongside me — I can't imagine how hard it must have been to do it alone.

Earhart suffered from icy conditions, heavy winds and technical problems with the plane, and was forced to land in Northern Ireland instead of France as she'd been planning — much to the surprise of some local farmers who weren't expecting her! She'd crossed the Atlantic successfully in just under 15 hours, becoming the first woman, and second person ever, to do it. But Earhart wasn't content with that — she had an even bigger journey in mind …

55

USA

Start

MIAMI

① On 1 June 1937, Earhart and Noonan departed from Miami.

PUERTO RICO

② Her plane was a Lockheed Electra 10E, modified to include extra fuel tanks and additional navigational equipment.

VENEZUELA

SENEGAL

④ Earhart reached Senegal on 8 June, setting a record for the fastest-ever crossing of the South Atlantic (13 hours and 22 minutes).

FORTALEZA
BRAZIL

③ Lots of stops were required to refuel the plane. In Fortaleza, Brazil, Earhart took an extended break so her aircraft could be checked.

AROUND THE GLOBE

56

Many explorers feel the urge to put their name in the history books, and Amelia Earhart was no different. When she turned 40, she set her mind on a final goal: to become the first woman to circumnavigate the globe by aircraft. She made a first attempt in March 1937, aiming to circle the world by going west. But her plane crashed on take-off in Hawaii, and had to be sent back for repairs. Finally, in June, she was ready to try again, aiming to fly 47,000 km along the equator. She had a navigator, Fred Noonan, with her, and some of the most sophisticated navigational equipment ever invented at that time. The whole world waited with bated breath: would the Queen of the Air succeed once more?

5 Taking off from Sittwe, Myanmar, on 18 June, Earhart was soon forced to turn back because of bad weather. When it improved, she took flight for Thailand.

6 In Indonesia, Earhart decided to take a three-day rest – she and Noonan needed it, and so did the plane! The whole aircraft got a major overhaul before she took off for Australia.

7 On 2 July, Earhart and Noonan took off from Lae, a town on Papua New Guinea in the Pacific Ocean. They were aiming for Howland Island, a small spit of land over 4,000 km away.

SITTWE
THAILAND
INDONESIA
PAPUA NEW GUINEA
LAE
AUSTRALIA

AN UNSOLVED MYSTERY

But Earhart never reached Howland Island. Apart from a few distress signals, the plane was never heard from or seen again. But Earhart was one of the most famous women in the world and the US president, Franklin D. Roosevelt, wasn't going to let her vanish. He spent $4 million sending out a search party to find her, but it was a huge area of ocean to cover. After two years of hunting, the search teams gave up and Amelia Earhart was announced as lost at sea. To this day, no one knows what happened to her, but her legacy as a fearless and intrepid pilot, and a pioneer of women's aviation, lives on.

57

MOUNT EVEREST
THE ULTIMATE PEAK

SUMMIT

5 At altitude, there is less oxygen in the air for the lungs to breathe, which makes climbing exhausting. The final hurdle Hillary and Norgay faced was a sheer rock face with steep cliffs on either side. They scrambled up it until, at last, they were standing on top of the world at a height of 8,848 m.

CAMP VII

CAMP VI B

Mount Everest, the tallest mountain in the world, doesn't stand alone. It is surrounded by other massive peaks, one of which I attempted to summit: Mera Peak. We had to turn back because some of the team got frostbite, which can lead to you losing whole fingers or toes. So I am in awe of a young New Zealander named Edmund Hillary who, in the spring of 1953, joined a British expedition attempting to summit Everest. He'd been obsessed with climbing since school and was fascinated by the idea of scaling the world's highest mountain. It wasn't long before the expedition set off across the shifting ice, navigating 200-m-deep crevasses, as Hillary forged a route through the challenging terrain.

2 The explorers built many camps on the side of the mountain so that they could come back to the safety and shelter of their tents if the weather got bad.

1 In the 1950s the climbers had basic radios and aviator sunglasses. The gear mountaineers take today is very different! However, ice axes, which are used to create a firm hold in the ice, have hardly changed in shape – though they are made from lighter metals these days.

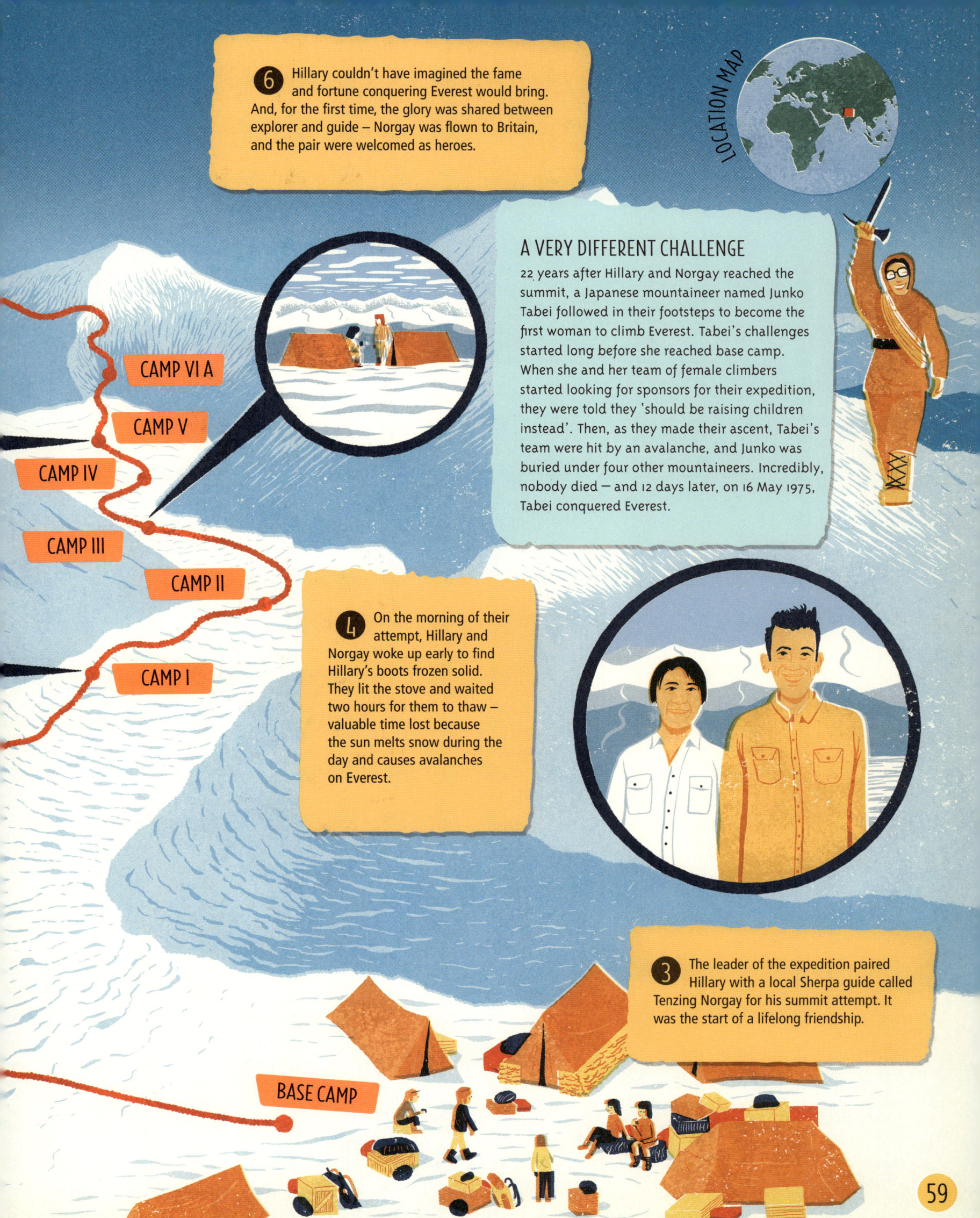

6 Hillary couldn't have imagined the fame and fortune conquering Everest would bring. And, for the first time, the glory was shared between explorer and guide – Norgay was flown to Britain, and the pair were welcomed as heroes.

LOCATION MAP

A VERY DIFFERENT CHALLENGE

22 years after Hillary and Norgay reached the summit, a Japanese mountaineer named Junko Tabei followed in their footsteps to become the first woman to climb Everest. Tabei's challenges started long before she reached base camp. When she and her team of female climbers started looking for sponsors for their expedition, they were told they 'should be raising children instead'. Then, as they made their ascent, Tabei's team were hit by an avalanche, and Junko was buried under four other mountaineers. Incredibly, nobody died – and 12 days later, on 16 May 1975, Tabei conquered Everest.

CAMP VI A
CAMP V
CAMP IV
CAMP III
CAMP II
CAMP I

4 On the morning of their attempt, Hillary and Norgay woke up early to find Hillary's boots frozen solid. They lit the stove and waited two hours for them to thaw – valuable time lost because the sun melts snow during the day and causes avalanches on Everest.

3 The leader of the expedition paired Hillary with a local Sherpa guide called Tenzing Norgay for his summit attempt. It was the start of a lifelong friendship.

BASE CAMP

59

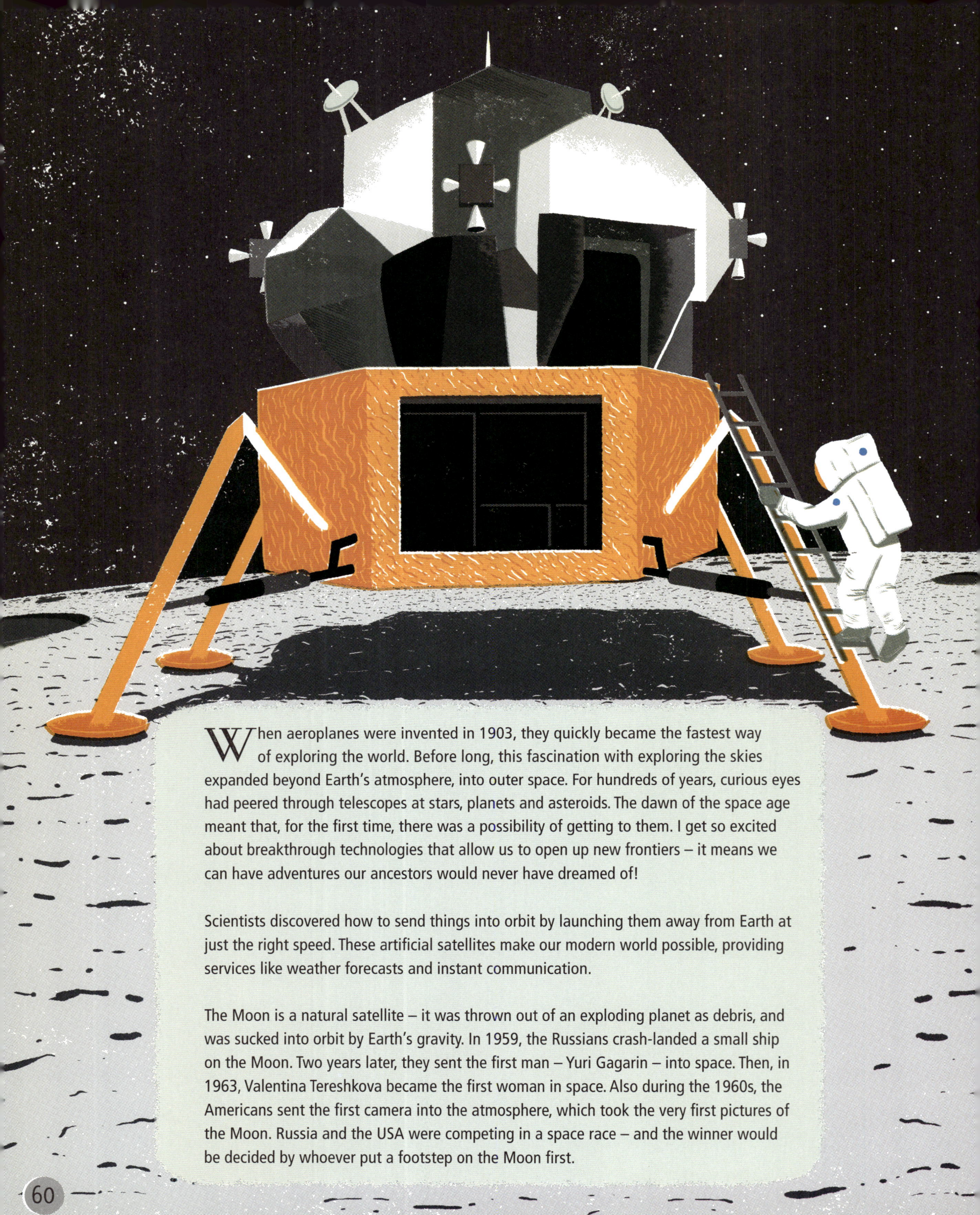

When aeroplanes were invented in 1903, they quickly became the fastest way of exploring the world. Before long, this fascination with exploring the skies expanded beyond Earth's atmosphere, into outer space. For hundreds of years, curious eyes had peered through telescopes at stars, planets and asteroids. The dawn of the space age meant that, for the first time, there was a possibility of getting to them. I get so excited about breakthrough technologies that allow us to open up new frontiers – it means we can have adventures our ancestors would never have dreamed of!

Scientists discovered how to send things into orbit by launching them away from Earth at just the right speed. These artificial satellites make our modern world possible, providing services like weather forecasts and instant communication.

The Moon is a natural satellite – it was thrown out of an exploding planet as debris, and was sucked into orbit by Earth's gravity. In 1959, the Russians crash-landed a small ship on the Moon. Two years later, they sent the first man – Yuri Gagarin – into space. Then, in 1963, Valentina Tereshkova became the first woman in space. Also during the 1960s, the Americans sent the first camera into the atmosphere, which took the very first pictures of the Moon. Russia and the USA were competing in a space race – and the winner would be decided by whoever put a footstep on the Moon first.

INTO SPACE
TO INFINITY AND BEYOND

That's one small step for man, one giant leap for mankind.

The Americans chose an astronaut called Neil Armstrong to lead their mission. Armstrong had been obsessed with flight all his life, gaining his pilot's licence at just 16 years old. After finishing his studies, he joined NASA to test rocket planes, and was later promoted to the space programme.

More than three years later, in 1969, he was strapped into the *Apollo 11* space vehicle with two other astronauts named Buzz Aldrin and Michael Collins. Destination: the Moon. The launch and journey went perfectly, and four days later Armstrong landed the vehicle on the Moon's surface. Staring at a sight that no person had ever seen before, he took his first steps on the dusty ground, saying into his radio, 'That's one small step for man, one giant leap for mankind.' He and Aldrin gathered scientific data, including rock samples, before voyaging back to Earth to land in the sea.

Neil Armstrong's words couldn't have been truer. In the years since, an International Space Station has been built out in the atmosphere, and new planets are being discovered all the time. Space exploration is only just beginning!

DIVING DOWN INTO
THE DEEP

It's strange to think that we know more about outer space than we do about the depths of our home planet. I've always loved scuba diving, discovering the unusual creatures and bizarre plants that live underwater. And I'm not alone – ever since the first sailors set sail across the seas, explorers have been curious about what lies beneath the surface. Magellan, the first person to circumnavigate the globe, tried to measure the Pacific Ocean's depth by dangling down a weighted line, but it didn't reach the bottom. When scientists eventually did find the sea floor, it was much deeper than anyone had imagined. In 1875, the deepest section of the ocean was discovered. It is almost 11,000 m deep – if you put Mount Everest on the bottom, its peak wouldn't break the water's surface – and is called the Mariana Trench. It is the least explored place on the planet.

James Cameron's Deepsea Challenge expedition used high-definition 3-D cameras to broadcast all over the world.

Exploring the unknown means overcoming the obstacles in each new environment. Mountain climbers struggle to breathe at high altitudes, so oxygen equipment was developed to assist summit expeditions. The problem for underwater explorers is that water pressure increases the deeper you go. At the bottom of the ocean, the pressure is strong enough to crush some metals! It has only been in the past 60 years or so that technology has advanced enough to make travelling right to the bottom of the sea possible.

In 1960, the first descent into the Mariana Trench was launched with a crew of two, Jacques Piccard and Don Walsh. Their metal submersible was strong enough to prevent them from being squashed. The sub reached the bottom of the ocean surrounded by pitch black darkness – light cannot penetrate so far down. Scientists thought that nothing could survive down there because the pressure is so high, but Piccard and Walsh saw sea cucumbers and a lot of really weird fish – there were enormous jellyfish, fish with lights sticking out from their heads, and creatures with such transparent skin you could see their organs!

It took another 52 years for a second manned sub to make it down into the trench, and this time Canadian filmmaker James Cameron was at the helm. His Deepsea Challenge expedition used high-definition 3-D cameras to broadcast the exploration all over the world. He took 80 hours of footage and conducted research into life hiding away in the depths. Scientists were amazed to discover microbes thriving there. Though these microbes are small – too tiny to see with the naked eye – discovering them was a huge breakthrough. The Mariana Trench just goes to show that there is still *so* much to explore on Planet Earth.

INDEX

A
Afghanistan 10, 13, 15, 25, 53
Africa 6, 8, 9, 24, 26, 28, 33, 35, 37, 45, 46, 47
Aldrin, Buzz 61
Alexander the Great 4, 17, 10–13
Alexandria 12, 13
America 30, 39
Americas, the 31, 34, 42
Amundsen, Roald 50
ancestors 6, 7, 60
Antarctica 37, 51
Apollo 11 61
Arabia 7, 8, 17
Arabian Peninsula 6, 49, 52
Armstrong, Neil 61
Asia 7, 20, 21, 24, 36, 34
Atlantic Ocean 30, 37, 55
Australia 7, 35, 57

B
Babylon 12, 13
Baghdad 18, 26, 27
Baker, Florence 44
Baker, Samuel 44
Baret, Jeanne 42
Bell, Gertrude 53
Bird, Isabella 52
Bivvy bag 23
Bly, Nellie 48–49
Brazil 6, 56
Britain 18, 49
Burton, Richard Francis 44–45

C
Cameron, James 62, 63
Canada 38, 55
Cape of Good Hope 32, 35
Caribbean 30, 32, 33
Ceylon 25, 26, 29
Chile 33, 41
China 7, 15, 21, 25, 26, 27, 28, 29
christianity 21, 41
church 25, 26
circumnavigate 32, 35, 42, 48, 49, 52, 57, 62
Clark, William 39
Collins, Michael 61
Columbus, Christopher 30–31, 32
Constantinople 25, 26
Cook, Captain James 4, 34–37

D
Damascus 24, 26
Darwin, Charles 40–41
de Dorantes, Esteban 42
Deepsea Challenge Expedition 63
Delhi 25, 26, 27
Dieulafoy, Jane 53
diplomat 11, 15, 21, 39, 53
Drake, Sir Francis 32–33

E
Earhart, Amelia 4, 54–57
Egypt 9, 10, 15, 49
Egyptians 8, 9
Emperor Darius III 14–15
Endurance 51
Ethiopia 45, 53
Europe 32, 53

F
France 7, 18, 20, 49, 55

G
Galápagos Islands 41
Germany 18, 20

H
Hajj 16, 17, 24, 26
Hawaii 37, 57
He, Zheng 28–29
Henson, Matthew 50
Hillary, Edmund 58–59
Himalayas 6, 23, 24, 26, 43
HMS *Beagle* 40
HMS *Endeavour* 34–35
HMS *Resolution* 37
Homo sapiens 6–7

I
Ibn Battuta 24–27
Iceland 30, 43
India 10, 13, 21, 25, 28, 29, 30, 53
indigenous 39, 42
Indonesia 21, 28, 29, 35, 57
Iran 15, 20, 28, 53
Iraq 18, 27, 53
Ireland 18, 30, 53
Italy 18, 20, 30, 49

K
Khan, Kublai 21
Kingsley, Mary 47

L
Lewis, Meriwether 39
Lindbergh, Charles 55
Livingstone, David 46–47

M
Macedon 10, 12
Magellan, Ferdinand 32–33, 62
malaria 13, 46, 52
Maldives 25, 36
Marina Trench 62–63
Mecca 16–17, 24, 26
Middle East 26, 52–53
Moon 60, 61
Morocco 24, 25
Mount Everest 43, 58
Murphy, Dervla 53

N
Nanjing 28, 29
New Zealand 35, 36
nomads 9, 17
Noonan, Fred 56–57
North America 6, 18, 43
Norgay, Tenzing 58–59

O
On The Origin of the Species 41
Oro 34

P
Pacific 32, 37, 38, 49, 57
Pakistan 17, 53
Peary, Robert 50
Persia 10, 15, 20, 53
Persian empire 10, 12–13
Pharaoh 9, 10, 14
Philippines 32, 33
Piccard, Jacques 63
pilgrim 16, 17
pilgrimage 17, 24, 26
Plymouth 33, 34
Polo, Marco 5, 20–21

R
River Nile 8–9, 24, 42, 45, 46
Roosevelt, Franklin D. 57
Russia 18, 25, 43, 60

S
Sacagawea 38, 39
sacrifice 16, 19
Sahara Desert 5, 9
Scott, Robert Falcon 22, 50
Shackleton, Ernest 22, 51
Shoshone 38–39
Silk Road 14–15, 20, 21
slaves 33, 38, 45
Snook, Neta 55
South America 6, 33, 40
South Georgia 51
South Pole 50–51
southern hemisphere 34
space 43, 60
Spain 18, 32
Speke, John Hanning 44–45
Sri Lanka 25, 26, 28, 29, 49
Stanley, Henry Moreton 46–47
Stark, Freya 52
Syria 10, 53

T
Tabei, Junko 59
Tahiti 34
Tangier 24, 26
Tereshkova, Valentina 43, 60
Terra Australis 34
Thailand 28, 57
Thorbjarnardottir, Gudridur 43
trade 8, 17, 11, 14, 15, 25, 29, 40, 46
Turkey 10, 21

U
United States of America 39, 60

V
Verne, Jules 48, 49
Vikings 4, 18–19, 43
Vostok 6 43

W
Walsh, Don 63
Weihenmayer, Erik 43

Z
Zam Zam 17
Zheng He 28–29
Zinc oxide tape 23

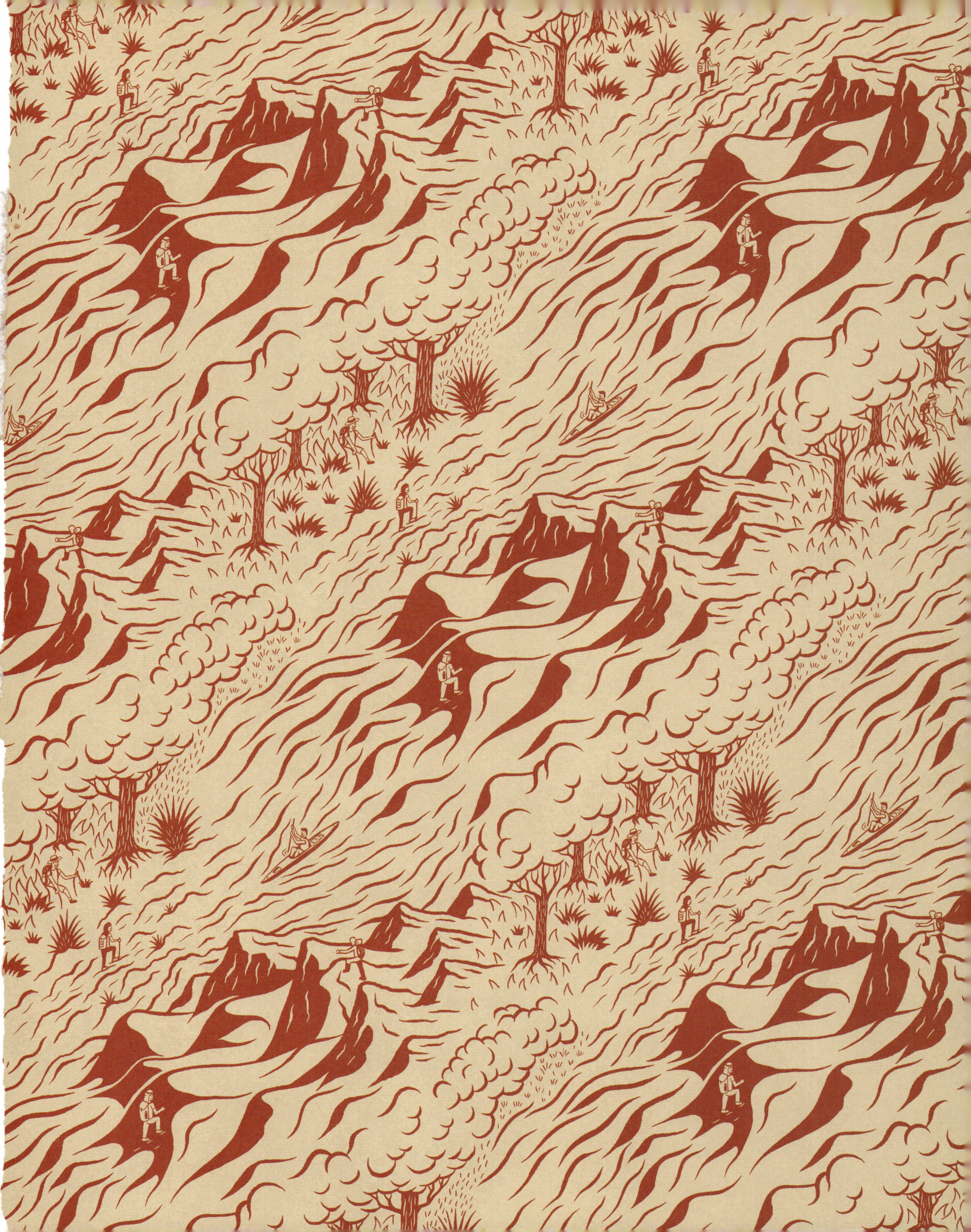